# Great Corporate Culture

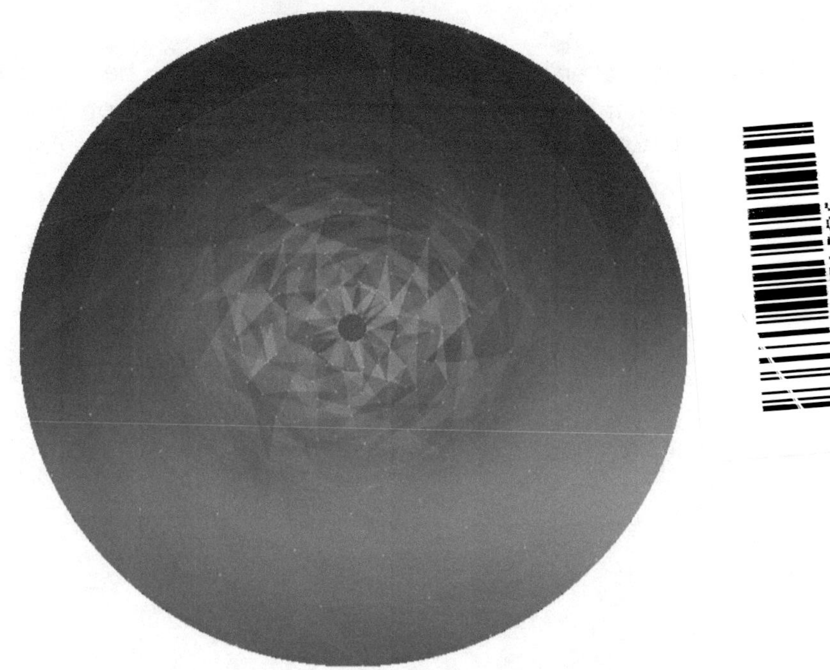

## The Ultimate Business Development Engine to Grow Earnings by 50+%

## A Strategy Handbook for Extraordinary Business Development

ISBN: 978-3-9525174-4-4

# Disclaimer

All characters, names, events, and incidents portrayed in this business development handbook are fictitious, but inspired by a variety of real experiences the author had or by other events that happened to real salespeople. No identification with products, places, buildings, or actual persons (deceased or living) is intended or should be inferred. Resemblance to anyone or any incident or place is purely coincidental.

# Contents

# <u>Acronyms and Definitions</u>

| | |
|---|---|
| Corporate Culture | Corporate culture refers to the beliefs and behaviours that determine how a company's employees and management interact and handle outside business transactions (Investopedia). |
| Business Model | A business model describes the rationale of how an organisation creates, delivers, and captures value in economic, social, cultural, or other contexts (Wikipedia). |
| CRM | **C**ustomer **r**elationship **m**anagement is an approach to managing a company's interactions with current and potential customers (Wikipedia). |
| ERP | **E**nterprise **r**esource **p**lanning is the integrated management of main business processes, often in real time and mediated by software and technology (Wikipedia). |
| KPI | **K**ey **p**erformance **i**ndicator (KPI) is a type of performance measurement. KPIs evaluate the success of an organisation or of a particular activity (such as projects, programs, products and other initiatives) in which it engages (Wikipedia). |
| PO | A **p**urchase **o**rder is the first official offer issued by a buyer to a seller indicating types, quantities, and agreed-upon prices for products or services (Wikipedia). |
| LE | A **l**arge **e**nterprise meets at least one of the following conditions: it has at least |

| | 5000 employees; or it has an annual turnover greater than 1.5 billion euros and a balance sheet total of more than 2 billion euros (Insee). |
|---|---|
| SME | **S**mall and **m**edium-sized **e**nterprises (SMEs) employ fewer than 250 persons and have an annual turnover not exceeding 50 million euro, and/or an annual balance sheet total not exceeding 43 million euro (Eurostat). |
| PE firms | A **p**rivate **e**quity firm is an investment management company that provides financial backing and makes investments in the private equity of start-ups or operating companies through a variety of loosely affiliated investment strategies including leveraged buyout, venture capital, and growth capital (Wikipedia). |
| M&A | **M**ergers & **a**cquisitions are transactions in which the ownership of companies, other business organisations, or their operating units is transferred or consolidated with other entities (Huxley). |
| Organisation | An organisation is an entity comprising multiple people, such as an institution, company, or association, that has a particular purpose (Wikipedia). |
| Affiliated Brands | This term refers to organisations that are owned and controlled by a separate, third party. |
| Sales Strategy | A sales strategy is a plan a business or individual makes to sell products and services and increase profits (Chron). |
| SOW | **S**hare **o**f **w**allet is a survey method used in performance management to measure how much of a company's |

| | |
|---|---|
| | spending on a certain product category goes to a particular business-to-business (B2B) vendor (Iammoulude). |
| Product managers | A product manager is the professional for the development of products for an organisation, known as the practice of product management (Wikipedia). |
| Project managers | Project managers have the responsibility for planning, procurement, and execution of a project in any undertaking that has a defined scope (Wikipedia). |
| OEM | An **o**riginal **e**quipment **m**anufacturer is a company that produces parts and equipment that may be marketed by another manufacturer (Seller Central). |
| Business Strategy | Business strategy can be understood as the course of action or set of decisions which assist entrepreneurs and executives to achieve specific business objectives (Business Jargons). |
| EMEA | EMEA is a shorthand designation meaning Europe, the Middle East, and Africa (Wikipedia). |
| Visual Communication | Visual communication conveys ideas and information in forms that can be seen, static and digital. These include signs, typography, drawing, graphic design, illustration, industrial design, advertising, animation, colour, and electronic resources (Wikipedia). |
| Operational Excellence | Operational excellence is the execution of an organisation's business strategy more consistently and reliably than the competition. It is determined by the results (BTOES). |
| Value Proposition | A promise of the value to be delivered. This term can apply to entire companies |

| | |
|---|---|
| | or individual products, and in the latter case, it is used by salespeople to close deals with their customers. |
| TR | A **t**echnical **r**epresentative gives advice on the application, installation, operation, and maintenance of an organisation's products, in addition to selling the products. In most organisations, salespeople manage the value proposition and negotiations to close the deal, while the technical representatives put the value proposition into physical practice. |
| SKU | In the field of inventory management, a **s**tock **k**eeping **u**nit (SKU) is a distinct type of item for sale, such as a product or service, and all attributes associated with the item type that distinguish it from other item types (Seller Central). |
| Sales Pipeline | Sales pipelines are forecasts of potential business opportunities that salespeople have identified to reach their sales quota. A sales pipeline illustrates where prospects or business opportunities are in the sales cycle. Their win probability is noted as a percentage, along with expected dates to close these deals. |

# Preface

Corporate culture means different things to different people. It is hard to view externally: the long-standing, implicitly shared values, beliefs, and assumptions that influence people's behaviour, attitudes, and meaning within an organisation.

This book explores corporate culture as a critical ingredient for an organisation's success or failure, particularly in the area of sales performance. Corporate culture is a complex construct, as the cover art illustrates, depicting the decentralised communication construct that's part of a productive corporate culture. This book's content seeks to inform, inspire, and prepare young salespeople (and future leaders) to be successful in one of the toughest jobs in the world. A stereotype, often negative, is still tied with being in sales, and this book will both challenge that prejudiced view and offer perspective and actionable information for salespeople at all levels of experience to succeed despite this and other obstacles. Like entrepreneurs, salespeople will experience rejection, defeat, and disappointment as part of their daily business. However, when salespeople develop the discipline to face these challenges head-on and master a positive mental attitude, these challenges will lose their power over them, and they will have a much easier time. These practices can especially help when a salesperson decides to become an entrepreneur or takes on another leadership position. Perhaps the most crucial reason why sales professionals make great leaders is that they tend to have a high degree of awareness and to understand that business isn't always about logic.

To complete my independent research on the affect corporate culture has on an organisation's sales performance, I needed to record one extreme case of a toxic workplace. Conducting extensive research, I spoke to salespeople from different industries to identify correlating factors, and I then evaluated the most extreme example of a toxic workplace. I came across numerous salespeople, some of the most pertinent being millennials in the digital business sectors, who had experienced some truly terrible work environments. When speaking with them, I quickly realised I was only scratching the surface of a much more significant challenge in the way organisations measure the link between corporate culture and sales performance today. It is particularly crucial in terms of accountability and sales performance, which when properly managed can create a happy workplace that rewards and brings out the best in all employees.

As I dug deeper, I found correlating factors that contributed to either a happy workplace or a toxic workplace. Existing employees, including new hires, expect a happy workplace, and leaders aim to deliver it, but who decides when they succeed? If an organisation is genuinely employee-centric, the answer is simple – the employee ultimately decides. However, we still see many toxic workplaces plagued with low levels of employee engagement. These organisations have accumulated a tradition in which hard work and input are valued over concrete outcomes. Employees then strive to look good in presentations and meetings, and they behave "smart" with information, but when leaders speak about these employees' key performance indicators, are they looking at their input alongside outcome, or do they value the employee's perceived IQ (intelligence quotient) factor over the actual results they have achieved? A genius IQ does not guarantee the delivery of high-quality results.

Meanwhile, great leadership, like great sales performance, is a combination of wisdom, compassion, and persuasion. Successful sales professionals have this unique understanding of the human element and embody this mix of skills in just the right amount at the right moment. This book will help young salespeople establish a competitive advantage as they develop their emotional intelligence alongside their strategic sales plans. It shares the adventures of salespeople who practiced due diligence even when their direct bosses were unwilling to recognise their performance as productive. The worst bosses actually take credit for the productive results achieved by these salespeople.

The conscientiousness of these employees and their courage as salespeople is truly inspiring. Although they have many odds against them, salespeople everywhere are still able to deliver sustainable year-on-year revenue growth. They generate double-digit millions for regional offices and put profit in the hands of investors. These salespeople are likely curious about the sales performance increase that can be achieved with a happy workplace, or on the contrary, the potential sales performance decline realised with a toxic workplace. This book offers such information.

The lesson-learned about a happy workplace is that it shortens product time to market and creates an efficient sales cycle. Its counterpart, the toxic workplace, elongates these factors, creating costly, lengthy product time to market and inefficient sales activities. A happy workplace is a vital success factor for overall sales performance, which is, in turn, a critical factor for the bottom-line success or failure of an organisation. The findings presented in this book reveal a drop in potential earnings of 50+% over thirty-six months with a toxic workplace, or on the contrary, a potential earnings increase of 50+% with a happy workplace. This percentage was measured from a sales department's perspective. Naturally, a happy work environment is sure to produce cost-effective benefits for other parts of the organisation as well. The economic investment to achieve a happy workplace is more than justified by the better engagement and collaboration that result. When a strategy is well-designed and executed from all parts of the organisation, it results in a positive return on investment. Product innovation includes a shorter product time to market, and increased revenue growth results from a shorter sales cycle. These benefits are so widely recognised that it has become increasingly common for larger corporations to institute a new role, the CCO: Chief Culture Officer. A full-time position is not necessary for most businesses, but an understanding of the dynamics involved will make any employee an asset to the health of their workplace, both socially and financially. This book offers a foundation.

Over the past twenty-five years, I've had the opportunity to meet thousands of working professionals from different vertical markets in Europe. My interest writing about corporate culture emerged after concluding twenty years of experience working in different sales roles in various vertical market industries where I amassed a total combined sales revenue in the three-digit millions for organisations working with various business models. I owe my track record as a strategist and business developer to my endless curiosity, reading many books on business strategy and effective sales performance, including *Take The Cold Out Of Cold Calling* by Sam Richter, *The Cold Calling Techniques* by Stephan Schiffman, and the Denison survey "Bringing Corporate Culture to the Bottom Line,"[1] which considers this crucial aspect in terms of return on investment and other financial indicators, and finds that companies with a participative culture reap an ROI nearly twice as high as firms with less efficient or engaged cultures. The data presented here provide hard evidence that the cultural and behavioural aspects of organisations are intimately linked to both short-term performance and long-term survival.

For the past two decades, I've been exploring the world of strategic business development, and now I want to share my knowledge with other curious readers. Today we see many studies, blogs, and books explaining corporate culture and the impact it has on the overall wellbeing of an organisation. Yes, these theories, statistics, and recommendation are relevant for the "big picture" of pros and cons. Still, there is an invaluable perspective that only comes from someone who has actually been at the forefront of these battles, as a

---

[1] https://www.researchgate.net/publication/13029854_Bringing_Corpo rate_Culture_to_the_Bottom_Line

business developer, and has directly experienced the positive and negative impact of different corporate cultures.

Despite the growing interest and body of research, there is still little reliable evidence about the potential revenue impact of an organisation's sales performance with a happy workplace or a toxic one. The evidence that a toxic workplace negatively impacts the balance sheet does exist, though it is seldom presented to convince organisations; therefore, corporate culture initiatives often remain a postponed consideration for leaders. This book provides such evidence, including a list of factors which have a negative impact on revenue in many organisations today.

There are internal and external factors that impact an organisation's' corporate culture performance. This manuscript discusses the internal factors and contributes to the case for greater attention, sharing new information and perspective on how corporate cultural (that is, a happy versus toxic workplace) is closely associated with an organisation's long-term survival. Results proposed here can contribute to further studies in the field of corporate culture's impact on business development performance.

# Prologue

Corporate culture is an integral part of our everyday life as business professionals. We have to embrace it to make the theory meaningfully applicable. Most can agree that corporate culture is a set of practices, behavioural principles, and beliefs that form the core of an organisation's true identity.

Studies going back to the 1980s explain the connections between corporate culture and productivity, including the role corporate culture plays in creating a competitive advantage. Yet, nearly forty years later, too many leaders are still unwilling or unable to choose among competing values, beliefs, and parties. This hesitation creates toxic workplaces that cost organisations millions in delayed revenues and missed or lost deals. A toxic workplace suffers from high employee turnover, and former workers may even file defamation suits, resulting in costly legal proceedings and harmful brand exposure.

In particular, private equity (PE) firms struggle the most to address corporate culture and create further profits for their investors. Rather than constructing value over the years among investors and leadership, and encouraging active investor governance through biannual or annual reviews, PE firms typically set long-term targets, often three to five years – meaning out of sight, out of mind. Lack of active investor involvement can be even more pernicious at times when guidance is most necessary, such as before and after mergers and acquisitions (M&A), which call for deliberate change management. This book will highlight examples of workplace environment impact pre- and post-M&A. Though M&A is intended to improve competitiveness, it's no secret that mergers tend to fail. Historically, roughly two-thirds of companies lose value on the stock market after a merger, and studies on the outcome of M&A also show that 30% fail within three years. Most of these failures are due to disparities in organisational culture and lack of change management. Generally, when M&A occurs, it brings a shift in leadership principles, practices, and strategies that will have all types of implications on the people in both organisations. A sudden shift in certain practices creates disruption and unease. It takes time for an M&A to happen, as employees seldom replace their underlying beliefs and values all at once. Only when the critical "people" aspect of the M&A has been considered for cultural fit can we be assured that combining the two companies makes sense.

Another related factor that affects bottom-line performance is the quality of the business model. Though corporate culture – the relationship between individuals and organisational performance – remains a key experiment for leaders, they too rarely re-evaluate their business model to find a way for their organisation to provide customers with more value than their competitors. A business model is a complementary element to the product features, benefits, and value an organisation delivers to its customers. It analyses a market segment's values, proposes products or services for that specific market segment, and shapes plans to enhance the business's capability and capacity to perform business activities within that market segment. Yet constant disruption from technology and innovation is making business models more vulnerable today than ever before. Although almost all business models eventually become obsolete, confusion and misunderstanding still surround the concept of them – a concept that could become the basis of additional competitive advantage.

Understanding the market segments' needs and incorporating them into the business model – plus periodically updating that model as the sector changes, customer demands change, or technology creates new opportunities and threats – will create a lasting competitive advantage.

For too long, corporate culture has been viewed as the responsibility of the human resource (HR) department rather than an integral part of business strategy. While HR is certainly part of the bigger picture, your first choice to build a happy workplace should not be your HR team. A CEO or leader sets the corporate culture, and they will always play a key role in deciding what the organisation's core values are. Their behaviour and communication style at the leadership level has the most significant impact for better or worse. This is why communication, along with responsibility and trust, is crucial for a happy workplace, and why leadership is even more pivotal than HR. Your corporate culture is more than just hiring the right people and retaining them. It's also about learning their individual influencing characters, which determine how they act on a day-to-day basis.

The fundamental ingredient in a corporate culture's design is a conclusion about the thoughts and behaviour of others. People make decisions based on their principles, values, and what they know or believe to be true. To take control of their corporate culture, organisations should delegate responsibilities appropriately and emphasise the creation of a unified, transparent, and engaging workplace with plenty of buy-in from investors, executives, the CEO, and the employees from all department levels. The right combination of senior leadership members and general staff from different parts of the organisation must complete their due diligence. These employees are the ones present at running the business and they understand how it works in practice. They have a better perspective and understanding of what other employees will or will not respond to than any leader ever could. Although some large corporations assign corporate culture responsibilities to a Chief Culture Officer (CCO), a full-time position is not necessary for most businesses. Nor, as mentioned, should your first choice be your HR team. Everyone cannot do everything in an organisation; therefore, breaking up the responsibilities is essential.

Meanwhile, it's often said that a happy workplace is a choice – great leaders foster environments where all employees, regardless of age, race, or gender, feel valued.

Organisations may have diversity programs that focus more on creating a diverse workforce than on the harder job of fostering inclusion. When businesses fail to actively make those outside the dominant zone feel welcome, they lose the insight that people with different backgrounds or experience can bring to the table. Additionally, when employees don't have basic guidelines around what is standard or relevant behaviour, the result is often confusion, redundancy, and impaired or even abnormal functioning.

A corporate culture that is agilely designed will remain crucial in the ever-changing business environment. Consider that millennials are projected to make up 75% of the workforce by 2030. As they and Gen-Xers take on leadership roles, replacing their baby boomer predecessors, organisations will be forced to reshape how they approach employee morale and culture. These new generations are challenging conventional thinking about the modern workplace. Rather than working in a well-paid job from 9-5, many are willing to sacrifice a higher salary to work within a culture aligned to their values, and when they don't feel emotionally attached to the culture, they probably won't stick around for long. However, working professionals' response to salary growth and opportunity advancement are considered top factors in employee retention. Meanwhile, negative work-life balance and inadequate corporate culture heavily contribute to decreased satisfaction levels at work. Research shows that through a supportive management approach, leaders can make an enormous difference in the overall experience employees have within an organisation – and to how likely they are to stay with the organisation. This necessary change is also a way to improve the company's position. Employee skills and a healthy workplace are worth more than an organisation's tangible assets. Unlike financial and physical ones, intangible assets are hard for competitors to imitate, which makes corporate culture a robust and sustainable competitive advantage that can be measured as a strategic asset. As just one example, in drawing these new employees and retaining existing ones, a happy workplace possesses an advantage over competitors.

In a happy workplace, departments create joint relationships for a smooth engagement process during the entire sales cycle, making the organisation productive and sales-ready. Corporate culture is an interconnected construction, a living entity, influenced by coordinated actions. At the same time, each department can be defined as a subunit culture in itself, with different priorities, a different set of key performance indicators (KPIs), norms, values, and beliefs. This is also true of each individual within the organisation. Each subunit wants to take charge of a situation; it works with its own culture and focuses on attaining its own annual KPI goals. Because of this, when a weak subunit limits corporate culture's performance, strengthening another subunit won't make the intertwined system stronger. The moment you try to optimise any one part of an organisation without optimising the others, that optimisation may pose challenges for those other subunits. Most of the work in corporate culture design is figuring out these interactions and trade-offs.

Many leaders still lack the motivation to understand or deal with these tricky fundamentals and how to master them. A toxic workplace often comes about from miscalculation. Mistakes and errors can occur in assessing the problems presented by the constant disruption of technology and innovation, and in assessing one's resources, new hires, and the lessons learned. A miscalculation, however, is not the only source of a toxic workplace; one can also come about when leadership actively avoids the hard work of crafting a happy workplace. Too often, when leaders are unwilling or unable to understand a situation, they prefer not to make any decision at all. Another challenge is the poor allocation of resources to achieve the goals that are decided on. Even when they are set, corporate culture objectives will be unsuccessful if lack of support makes them impracticable, or if they fail to address truly critical issues.

A toxic workplace does not arise simply from the absence of a code of conduct. Instead, it grows out of specific misconceptions and leadership dysfunction. It is often exasperated by a blurry realm of doublespeak and can lead to high employee turnover rates. The working environment has a tense and hopeless atmosphere in which leaders are not held accountable and power struggles result in an extremely counterproductive situation. Despite an organisation's best efforts to build a productive corporate culture, too often, leaders end up creating a toxic workplace for their employees, and these employees have no ability to – or are afraid to – speak up. While leaders seem to get the job done, the top executives don't see a problem or the need to promote ways for employees to address issues and bring them to their attention. Organisations with a productive corporate culture don't tolerate leaders who achieve their business objectives at the cost of others. In fact, organisations that want to construct and uphold a productive corporate culture don't tolerate anyone who works towards outcomes that are not aligned with that desired culture.

Once you develop the ability to detect a toxic workplace, you will dramatically improve your effectiveness in judging, influencing, and growing your happy workplace. If you have a special insight or skill for removing the limiting factors that weaken a workplace, you have an advantage.

Many organisations, most of the time, don't have any corporate culture design. Instead, they have multiple goals and initiatives that symbolise progress but fail to come together. These organisations lack any approach to accomplishing that progress other than investing more and trying harder. If employees aren't happy, the organisation probably won't be successful. Corporate culture reveals the truth about employees' job satisfaction, motivation, and performance. The reason corporate culture is described as being "designed" is to emphasise the role of adjustments. In design problems where various elements are planned, adjusted, and coordinated, there can be quick wins to getting combinations right and sharp costs when getting them wrong. Making the wrong choice among competing values, beliefs, and parties is a contributing factor that puts the organisation at a standstill.

A happy workplace has many correlations in its design. It coordinates principles, policies, and resources while putting them in action to accomplish the end in mind (EIM). Corporate culture is the best business growth engine. Plus, an insightful reframing of your workplace situation brings out new patterns to identify advantages or weaknesses.

Trends and challenges are forcing organisations, PE firms, investors, and executives to re-evaluate their business strategy to ensure their corporate culture, their business model, and their sales strategy are still attractive for their intended purpose. This book offers a foundation from which the individual salesperson can contribute to that evaluation as they report to their leaders and advise on potential risks, weaknesses, and opportunities. In this way, the contributions of people at all levels will come together to establish a happier workplace.

<u>Part I</u>

# Happy Workplace / Toxic Workplace

# Chapter 1

## Corporate Culture: A Necessity

It's increasingly evident that a toxic workplace hampers all measures of success for an organisation. In particular, it hampers the bottom line when it puts a drag on employee productivity and innovation. Any change in your profits comes from your employees. When leadership listens to them, they will provide feedback that creates continued productivity. Engagement means employees flourish.

However, while engagement is a positive experience and has its benefits, many have noticed that when we are highly engaged in working, we also experience high levels of stress. When employee engagement is high, organisations may risk losing their most motivated employees because of high stress and burnout. In at least nine European countries, burnout is recognised as an occupational disease. While efforts have revolved around how to promote employee engagement, we also need to re-evaluate this approach, finding a way to avoid burning out employees in the process. The higher the workload and demands, the more support, acknowledgement, and opportunities for recovery the employee needs. While an organisation's wellness programs, like fitness and yoga, or the free stuff like drinks, fruit, and barbecues can be helpful, they are not the primary way to respond to that stress because a much more significant source of tension remains the workload itself and how it is managed.

Leaders and employees strive for smart engagement that leads to enthusiasm, motivation, and productivity, not burnout. To develop an optimal level of engagement, it is crucial to provide employees with success factors. These are the resources they need to do their job well, to feel worthy about their work, and to recover from the stress they experience through work. Also, leaders can re-evaluate their engagement processes during the entire sales cycle by asking employees how and where they can improve productivity, enhance performance, and increase engagement to raise retention levels. Instead of looking at tools for answers, leadership must look at people. When a lack of coordination between subunits weakens performance, the objective should be to promote dialogue and create a plan of action towards unblocking the bottleneck.

Leaders today are trying so hard to keep up that it's hard to slow down to make fundamental changes. They fail to create time in which to reassess strategies, much less to make necessary but fundamental changes to the way they acquire, maintain, and develop their employees and customers. Many organisations make statements about desired outcomes. The flaw is when they do this instead of having specific plans for overcoming obstacles. They pursue multiple objectives that are unconnected with each other, or worse, that conflict with one another.

A clear sense of priorities and disciplined focus is required because the more dynamic a challenging situation is, the poorer the foresight. In these situations, flexibility is essential. The more uncertainty exists, the more short-term objectives an organisation must have.

When putting all the pieces together, it all comes down to strategy. In a game of chess, a piece must be moved into a position that increases its playing options, while at the same time decreasing the flexibility and operations of the opponent's pieces. It's the same in business: pick objectives that put you in a position to increase your options relative to your competition. Consider such a goal now. Regardless of your organisation type: what single, feasible overall objective, when accomplished, would give you the most options and make the most significant difference in your overall business performance? How does this objective impact targets and indicators throughout your organisation's subunits?

For example, salespeople are pushed to achieve annual sales KPI targets, but what plans are in place to speed up product time to market (TTM) in a sustainable manner so that it continues to improve for the long term? Considering that nearly 80% of new products miss their target launch date, an organisation's product development team has enormous potential to reduce the new product TTM period. Achieving TTM goals generates more sales and profitability. It automatically shortens the sales cycle and enables salespeople to close more deals within a financial year. However, if the organisation lacks an action plan to speed up product time to market, this creates a bottleneck of transactions in the sales pipeline that salespeople cannot close, resulting in lower sales KPI achievements for that financial year.

Sometimes conflicting or split objectives come about because different departments in an organisation have different priorities. For example, an efficient credit & collections process is as valuable for the sales department as it is for the finance department because both departments want customers to settle payments on time. However, a workforce with a strong sense of customer experience is worth far more to the sales department than it is to the finance department, which, unfortunately, is sometimes reflected in how the finance department allots resource budgets. Another prioritisation challenge salespeople face is that many organisations use the same presales resources to close deals for both regional and international sales teams. Naturally, this creates a conflict of interest between regional and international business opportunities because they are in constant competition for those limited resources. The criteria by which an organisation can allocate these scarce resources in a productive way can be tricky to determine. It's my belief that organisations need to concentrate on corporate culture, make it a priority, and trust that other important issues will be taken care of automatically.

Many leaders have accepted that a happy workplace profoundly improves growth. They understand that ensuring employee goals are realistic, balanced, and supported with the appropriate resources will contribute to their achievement in a sustainable way. They persistently work to understand their corporate culture's challenges, own them, and calibrate it to address them. A general rule used in strategy design is: *Plan for the long term, but begin with short-term objectives; fail fast and scale quick.*

Let's examine an example of smart corporate culture with the Amazon acquisition of Zappos.

## Smart Corporate Culture Design

One of the most strategic leaders of our generation, Jeff Bezos, is well-known for his approach to ensuring shareholder value. It originated in the 1990s when Amazon began investing in long-term market leadership rather than short-term profitability. Over nearly twenty-five years in business, it has taken on an assertive acquisition strategy, buying up dozens of different companies. It worked: Amazon has overtaken Google and Apple to become the world's most valuable brand. Now Amazon is consistently in the news as the world's largest internet company by revenue.

Like anyone, Jeff can be wrong, but he insists on being challenged because that is when he gets a wide range of ideas brought to the table – both about change and how to manage it. Jeff has made it safe for the people surrounding him to challenge his decisions. He also thanks them for successful and unsuccessful ideas equally as they contribute to the culture process. Jeff doesn't care about being wrong personally. It's more important that his team gets to the right answers that keep the business pointed in the right direction. He has created a system that most of the time gets things right on the first try. In an interview with CNBC,[2] Bezos said

---

[2]https://www.cnbc.com/2017/11/06/the-surprising-trait-jeff-bezos-looks-for-in-successful-employees.html

of the employees Amazon hires, "I don't care how smart they are. I want to see a track record of hard decisions that ended up being right. It's always better in business to be right than smart – smart people can be wrong a lot." In other words, he gives job opportunities to people with a track record, and he listens to them even when their opinion of the right move challenges Jeff's own viewpoint. He surrounds himself with talented people who produce results instead of contributing inputs.

Jeff is highly intelligent; he thinks about details and a ten-year plan at the same time. I think that is what makes him stand out. He has mastered how to identify behaviours associated with the quality of conscientiousness that results in workplace success. For example, in 2009, a deal was sealed: Amazon acquired retailer Zappos for $1.2 billion. The purchase documents specified that Zappos's corporate culture would be kept unchanged and operated separately from Amazon.

Zappos is about excellent customer service. In 2010, CEO Tony Hsieh released a bestseller called *Delivering Happiness*, detailing how he runs the company with happiness in mind. Long before the 2009 acquisition, Zappos had functioned as an incubator for testing theories about corporate culture structure and productivity, even before "corporate culture" became the buzzword we see today. Much of the credit lies within Hsieh and his book.

Bezos's top priority was to understand Zappos's culture. As the richest man in the world, he knows that leaders cannot pay for loyalty. They must help employees connect to their core identity to transform their mindset. During recruitment, Zappos conducted a culture fit interview which carried half the weight of whether a candidate was hired. All employees, from executives to low-level administrative workers, must go through the same four-week call centre training where the company's ten core values were instilled. At the end of the first week, Tony Hsieh paid new hires $3,000 to quit if they decided that it wasn't what they expected. Zappos has been using holacracy and self-management since 2014. It moved away from the system design used by most organisations, which involves taking control and trying to predict and plan, towards a system that decentralises management and organisational governance. Zappos's departments are independent, self-organised, and self-managed. Authority and decision-making are calibrated on an ongoing basis by a leadership committee. In today's economic climate, Zappos looks for long-lasting business growth and success. In a hundred years, it shouldn't matter who the CEOs or presidents were, as long as the organisation's corporate culture they constructed will be resilient and stand the test of time.

Organisations around the world want to bring profit, passion, and purpose to their workplace, but some still struggle even to start. An organisation's operational excellence addresses the needs of its customers. It aims to ensure an efficient response to changes in customer behaviour and to develop solutions tailored to various customer segments. Corporate culture initiatives should foster capacity for change management, employee engagement, good leadership, and effective communication. Close collaboration between departments will ensure that customers get access to the organisation's full range of products and services.

A customer experience that delivers happiness has to be designed, implemented, and then recalibrated as necessary when it diverts from its intended course. This was the case at Zappos and with Amazon, who served as pioneers of smart corporate culture. They used the principle of happiness and over fifteen years of experience to create a profitable, sustainable, and healthy workplace. Zappos still holds its crowdsourced Ten Core Values:

1. Deliver WOW Through Service

2. Embrace and Drive Change

3. Create Fun and A Little Weirdness

4.  Be Adventurous, Creative, and Open-Minded

5.  Pursue Growth and Learning

6.  Build Open and Honest Relationships With Communication

7.  Build a Positive Team and Family Spirit

8.  Do More With Less

9.  Be Passionate and Determined

10. Be Humble

# Chapter 2

## Entering a New Workplace

In this chapter, we will begin to look in depth at the story of one millennial, Margaret. Her findings quantified a potential euro value for the cost of an extremely toxic workplace. In terms of missed revenue growth, this resulted in an astonishing 50+% loss over a thirty-six-month period for the sales department alone. The percentage doesn't include the impact the toxic workplace had on other departments. Her findings confirm that even though most organisations understand the effect a happy workplace has on their success, leaders still struggle to deliver the right culture fit. As a result, they lose revenue daily. At the same time, they delay enhancements and innovations that could produce higher efficiency, better productivity, and a greater positive impact from existing processes and practices.

Many organisations have experienced incredible growth over the past few decades. Acquisitions by PE firms have led to even faster growth, with some organisations going from hundreds of employees to thousands. As a young job seeker invited to interview at one such company, no doubt you would be thrilled, but keep in mind that no matter how grand the opportunity, you should pay attention to warning signs. The growth of happiness in the workplace has not always kept pace with the economic boom. Therefore, before taking on a new job, your number one priority should be to examine the culture fit, because you want to make sure the organisation has the right fit for you. Ask employees why they enjoy working there. What drives them to get up every morning, and what encourages them to stay at the organisation for so long? If you see that the corporate culture matters and passion manifests at every level, only then should you decide if you want to be a part of it. The decision to accept a job is an emotional one that ought to be driven by a corporate culture fit. At the end of the day, you want to feel that the organisation and employees, especially leaders, will resonate with your core values. This is not only a matter of emotion, though, but also of strategy. Since a toxic workplace will hobble sales performance, salespeople need to research the company for evidence of a corporate culture that fits their goals for themselves and their career.

## The Interview

The story begins in Wallonia, April 2012. Margaret applied for a sales manager role in Belgium's Wallonia region at a large enterprise (LE) organisation. Four weeks after submitting her application, Margaret was thrilled to receive an email invitation for her first face-to-face interview in Wallonia. She researched and prepared herself for the opportunity, including creating a well-thought-out sales proposal that included a 90–180-day plan she intended to present during the interview. In her research, she learned that the globally operating organisation was established fifty years before and had become a global leader in the field of visual communication. For over half a century, it advised and supplied Fortune 500 customers as well as those from the public sector, small and medium-sized enterprises (SMEs), and large corporations on a regional, national, and international basis. She also learned the organisation had been made up of roughly 110 employees when, one year before she applied for this position, it was acquired by a large private equity (PE) firm. As a result, the organisation grew to a workforce of nearly 1,000 employees throughout almost a dozen affiliated brands. Their headquarters was in the US while offices were stationed in Europe, the Middle East, and Africa (EMEA) with Italy as the EMEA headquarters.

On the day of the interview, a thrilled Margaret arrived on time at the Wallonia office. The company logo was on the building, and she entered through the front doors. With her mind on the interview, she took the elevator to the fifth floor as instructed in her email. On the fifth floor, she walked out of the elevator and stood in front of a dull grey door, with no logo, no window, and no information. When she tried to enter, she found the door was locked. Perplexed, she took the lift to a lower floor and spoke with another organisation's receptionist, who kindly let Margaret know that she needed to go to the fifth floor. When Margaret informed her that she had already been there, the receptionist joined her in her confusion. "They are located in another organisation's warehouse, and you need to go through that warehouse to get to them. Once you do, you'll come upon a door with a common laboratory sign." Margaret began to wonder about the professionalism of this company and even to doubt her decision to interview.

The receptionist knew someone who worked in the warehouse, so she phoned them to help Margaret gain access. Margaret thanked her and went back up to the fifth floor. Although this seemed quite unusual, she tried to keep an open mind as she made her way through the warehouse. Once she arrived in front of the door with the laboratory sign, she looked around for anything that proved she was in the right area. There were no company logos or symbols indicating so. Sceptical, she knocked before entering a space equipped with four office workplaces.

Margaret was welcomed by Rachael, who was the Vice President of the organisation. She introduced herself as the Head of Operations and led Margaret through the small office. Rachael was an elderly lady with glasses, dressed professionally in a black business suit and white blouse. She next introduced Margaret to Paul, the CTO (Chief Technology Officer). Paul was a young, tall, slim man, casually dressed. Rachael and Paul both had their workspaces in the Antwerp office and had only come to Wallonia for the interview. Margaret met three other employees who were part of the Wallonia office team. Her overall impression had grown more encouraging, and she found the office space, from the inside, satisfactory for a working environment, with soft, clear lighting and tasteful furnishings and decoration.

For the interview, Rachael and Paul led Margaret into a small conference room located at the end of the office. Rachael opened the discussion, and both technical and behavioural questions were asked. Margaret listened attentively as Rachael explained the roles and responsibilities of the position. Margaret thanked her for sharing those insights, then asked questions like:

a) What concerns and challenges did the organisation face?

b) What were the top three priorities they expected the right candidate to deliver in the next twelve months?

c) What were the day-to-day expectations and responsibilities of the job?

d) How would leadership measure her responsibilities and performance?

e) What were the sales quotas to achieve?

f) What benefits came with this position?

These seemed like fair and necessary questions to ask, but neither Rachael nor Paul could clearly answer them. Margaret went on to ask about the induction training program, including continued product training. Paul explained that regular training would be provided. The time came when Margaret was permitted to present her sales proposal. She was excited to offer her ideas and show what value she could bring to the organisation. Halfway through the presentation, however, she noticed Paul was disengaged. He began looking at his computer and answering her comments passively. This gave Margaret the impression that Paul's management style wasn't up to par, that he had higher priorities than being bothered with an interview – or even worse, he was simply bored with the research Margaret presented, or his disengagement was intentionally meant to distract her during the presentation. Still, she kept her focus and her enthusiasm and presented her proposal in its entirety to Rachael, who seemed pleased with its conclusion. Upon her interview's end, Margaret thanked both of them for their time and left the building. On her way home, she reflected on how it went, what she could have done differently, and also what could have caused Paul's disengagement during her presentation. Overall, she was pleased with her performance and felt confident that there would be a second interview.

Four days later, Rachael sent Margaret an email requesting a second interview, this time in Antwerp with the CEO and Margaret's potential future boss. The second interview date was set for two weeks later. When she arrived that day, Paul accompanied her to the CEO's office on the eighth floor of the organisation's building in Antwerp. He knocked on the door, and they both entered a nicely furnished office with a grey carpet and windows from ceiling to floor that offered a beautiful view of the Scheldt River. A large oak conference table stretched across the room, and a middle-aged gentleman sat at it in front of his laptop. The moment Margaret was in his company, he stood and greeted her with a firm handshake. "Hi, my name is Brad! It's so nice to meet you! Please take a seat." Margaret enthusiastically sat at the conference table with her back to the window.

Paul left the office, and Brad kicked off the interview with some small talk. During the interview, Margaret found him very friendly, pleasant, and humble in his personality. For nearly an hour, he provided insights on what he expected from her if she was chosen as the ideal candidate. She acknowledged and understood Brad's concern about developing the business further in the Wallonia region. She was eager to learn more about the topics which Rachael and Paul had not been able to address during the first interview. When a question on benefits arose, Brad informed her of a salaried sales position available. "We have a budget for this sales position but offer no incentive or bonus structure," he said. "I am in the works of implementing a sales bonus structure for all of my sales managers in EMEA, but we can't offer anything at this time."

It was an unfortunate aspect of the job that Margaret noted, but she was unemployed, as Brad knew. She wasn't willing to lose the potential job. Instead, she continued to stay positive, figuring she would probably be offered incentives when they were implemented in EMEA soon. Margaret felt like the right candidate for the position and had to trust that once she proved her value to the organisation, better benefits would surely follow. To avoid the risk of not being selected for the position, she didn't continue negotiations for other benefits. She would later come to regret that decision, as she learned that she had been one of the few who applied for the job offer and the best qualified for the sales position.

At the end of the interview, Margaret stood confidently, thanked Brad for the opportunity, and concluded by reaffirming her commitment to the organisation's success. He giggled as she shook his hand, which in her opinion was rather peculiar and came across as uncaring, but since the interview itself went well, she didn't put too much emphasis on his reaction.

Brad stood up only when Rachael appeared in the doorway. "Rachael will be in touch with you within the next few days," he said to her with a dismissive smile. Rachael waited in the doorway and escorted her out of the building.

With a week to ponder on Brad's reaction after what she felt was a successful interview, she was pleased when Rachael called her to sign a contract with them. The entire process had involved eight weeks of research, questions, discussions, and waiting. Margaret was overwhelmed yet excited to have been selected as the right-fit candidate for the sales manager position in Wallonia.


## The Induction Training Program

After a few days of working at her new job, Margaret was introduced to Miriam, who was assigned to train her for the sales position. Miriam was much older than Margaret, in her late fifties perhaps, and wore a charcoal grey business suit and crisp white blouse accented with a beautiful gold necklace. Although she seemed forthcoming, Margaret noticed that Miriam was also modest and unobtrusive. She did not discuss success factors she'd had with specific customers or within the organisation. Nor did she share challenges, even though such information would have been useful – in some cases, vital – for Margaret's success. Margaret also noticed that Miriam wasn't too willing to share specific details about the position. She was interested in Miriam's experience when it came to what worked well for her and looked forward to expanding on the strong points while avoiding or mending the weaker points with customers and within the organisation. However, for some reason, Miriam seemed to avoid interacting with Margaret as much as possible, and Margaret was unable to initiate such a conversation.

During the three-day handover period, Miriam and Margaret visited only two customers out of nearly one hundred in the Wallonia region. As a new employee, Margaret was grateful for the job opportunity, but at the same time, she would have liked to have a good foundation to work from. This included a better understanding of how Miriam worked in the office, how she interacted with customers, and how she coped with challenges within the group of affiliated brands. Margaret was aware that she was taking Miriam's position, not working with her or under her. However, Margaret didn't know then that Miriam was leaving the organisation in just a few days. A three-day handover for a sales professional was something Margaret had never experienced before or even heard of. Upon reflection, it seemed strange that Miriam would leave the organisation only a few years before her retirement. Although it wasn't an immediate concern, Margaret couldn't help but ponder the reasons.

She encountered other oddities as well. Margaret was disappointed to hear Miriam had left the organisation with her laptop containing all her work, including sensitive customer data and additional pertinent information. The data which salespeople gathered from customers was not appropriately logged since the organisation didn't have a customer relationship management (CRM) software system in place. Any customer contact information or details were either in an Excel spreadsheet or in OneNote, with no sales pipeline existing. The organisation had recently implemented Pega CRM in their US headquarters, but the EMEA leadership was still considering alternative tools such as SugarCRM.

Margaret later learned that two years prior, Miriam had won a tender, but the commissioning of this project was still ongoing. In Margaret's handover from Miriam, she found there wasn't much customer data history to look back on. She was concerned that Miriam didn't provide details around all pending project implementations. Consequently, she had to decide between continuing to build with the little information she had or developing a brand-new business development strategy. Due to the limited data, she chose to scrap the existing business development strategy and move forward with a new one, primarily focused on customer data management. She committed herself to learning everything she could in the first twelve months – including the key decision-makers of her top customers, their decision-making processes, their installed base, and their concerns and challenges. After each customer visit, Margaret would then create a meeting report. Each report document contained four sections:

(i) Attendees present at the meeting (including roles and contact details).

(ii) Meeting objective – why did the meeting take place?

(iii) Achieved outcome – what information was gathered?

(iv) Next steps – what will the salesperson and customer do after the meeting?

After completing the report, Margaret would archive it, giving access to other employees within the organisation. Meeting reports would also be sent to Brad and other employees who needed to be informed. This information flow would keep management updated on Margaret's sales activities, both those completed and those in progress.

After a week on the job, Margaret was invited to a six-day induction program that took place at the Antwerp office.

When she arrived there, Paul gave her a tour in which she was introduced for the first time to many of the employees and departments of the organisation. Margaret then approached different employees to begin her induction program. During the program, she met Steve, an internal salesperson with additional duties in the order processing and customer care departments. He was a middle-aged gentleman with a long beard and a shaved head. Everyone Margaret met during the induction program seemed underwater with heavy workloads, but Steve, in particular, looked at the edge of burnout. He ended up leaving the organisation six months later after being admitted into a burnout-program clinic. Margaret later learned that Steve was not the only employee who was admitted to such a clinic after leaving the organisation in exhaustion. Whether the workplace is to blame in these cases remains subject to countless debates, but given Margaret's own experiences, it does not seem unlikely.

Margaret found that Steve spent over half of his time updating Excel tables for invoicing purposes. Also, in some instances, when he received a customer's purchase order (PO), he didn't know what the customer ordered, because the PO did not reference a proposal number, nor did it include a stock-keeping unit (SKU) number as a reference. Consequently, rather than merely receiving the PO and processing it in the enterprise resource planning (ERP) system, Steve had to spend time looking up details of the customer's PO to get a better understanding of what was ordered. He often had to revert to the salesperson to get details on the order or return to the project managers and product managers with these clarification questions.

This problem came about because the ERP tool that the organisation used could only produce proposals for spare parts. This was ideal for the cosmetic or food sectors, but not suitable for the visual communication sector in which the organisation worked. It meant that no proposal for an end-to-end solution configuration with various components could be developed using it. This left Steve with a miscellany of activities to qualify the technical feasibility of an end-to-end solution before purchase orders could be internally processed. The organisation had purchased the wrong ERP tool. It was only able to do part of the job needed for a successful sales operation.

This situation was all new to Margaret. She knew that usually when salespeople send out pricing to customers, they send accurate proposals in which a technical or engineering specialist controls the technical configurations of the end-to-end solution. Thus, when the customer submits their PO, it contains the proposal number as a reference, and so the order processing team can book the customer's PO internally. Given this information, Margaret made it her mission to ensure that all customer POs coming from her Wallonia region were accurate. She planned to achieve this by involving a technical or engineering specialist to check the accuracy of the configuration during the presales phase before the final proposal was submitted to the customers. As a result, when back-office employees like Steve received a purchase order from Margaret's region, they would require much less time to process it. However, due to the ERP tool's limitations, this meant that Margaret would be using her time on what was not necessarily a sales activity. It was essential for her to step up to address this challenge so her region would deliver higher productivity, but the fact that she had to do so was itself a warning sign.

After the six-day induction program, in which Margaret had the opportunity to touch and feel a few existing products, she had not yet been able to receive software training. She thought that training would come later, but she didn't expect to wait too long since the software was part of the products she positioned in her regional market. Additionally, in any company, software and hardware training from the product management team must be continuous to help employees learn new features during new product launches. However, even though Margaret requested the software training several times over the following ten months, she had only one occasion to see two of the six software modules in a live demo. During the course of her training, or lack thereof, Margaret's previous experience working with different software platforms suggested to her that this organisation had serious software development and innovation challenges. This was not only because very few customers had purchased this software after its first version went live nearly two years before the M&A. It was also because, out of over 1,000 employees in the group, including almost 300 developers and engineers, only a handful could clearly explain and demo the software in front of a customer. Out of all EMEA sales regions, only two salespeople could somewhat explain or even demo a few modules of the software.

That was not the only problem. Software is only as good as its graphical user interface (GUI). If the GUI is not well executed, whether because the software platform is complicated or merely ill-designed, people will have trouble using the software. This certainly appeared to be the case with Margaret's new employer's software. She thought she might not have asked the right questions in the beginning, but her overall opinion thus far was that the company showed evidence of poor operation and innovation development, not to mention the part where specific training never took place. No training material was provided, and although she would have been happy to share her thoughts so the process could improve, no feedback was requested from new hires after the induction program.

# Chapter 3

## A New Hire's First Impression

### Adequate Tools to Do the Job

A few weeks before she left the organisation to be replaced by Margaret, Miriam had planned a meeting with a top customer in her French-speaking region. Margaret took on this meeting as part of her duties handed over from Miriam. On the day of the meeting, Margaret arrived on time, but the project manager assigned to this customer was nowhere to be seen. She called him, but he didn't answer. She then called Paul, who explained that the project manager was ill and advised Margaret to attend the meeting on her own. Margaret chalked it up to a lack of communication and talked herself into her first meeting alone.

She approached the reception desk at the customer site and asked to speak to Mr Harrison. Mr Harrison arrived shortly after, greeted her, and guided Margaret to a meeting room where his legal counsel and procurement had been waiting. The meeting's objective was to discuss specific stipulations of the service-level agreement (SLA) that Miriam sent a few weeks before she left the organisation. Margaret came unprepared for this meeting due to a lack of information and communication throughout her organisation. Although she was fluent in French, the language of the SLA, she was unaware that Miriam had sent an SLA to this customer and was unable to examine the stipulations before the meeting. Nor had she been aware that the meeting objective was to discuss these stipulations with their legal counsel.

Margaret gracefully informed the customer that she would record all stipulations that needed to be reviewed and revert with feedback or with a revised version of the SLA. They reviewed over a dozen different stipulations that needed a better understanding. After the meeting ended, Margaret left the customer site and returned to the office, nearly two hours away. As had become usual, she wrote a report to Brad about her meeting with the customer. She then went over the discussed stipulations, made amendments, and sent the SLA in French to Brad with a request that it be reviewed by legal counsel to safeguard the organisation's interests. A few days later, Brad came back to Margaret with the request to first translate the SLA from French to English so he could get a better understanding of the terms and conditions. Margaret told him that the translation was not a problem, but they would still need to get it revised by legal counsel.

Days and weeks passed, but Margaret didn't hear back from Brad. She did a follow-up call to check if he had given the SLA to legal counsel for review and hopefully approval. She even proposed a legal counsellor she knew in Wallonia, who spoke five different languages and already worked on SLAs for the visual communication sector. Brad reiterated the need for translation, leaving it now in Margaret's hands.

Margaret understood Brad's point about the translation because many of the organisation's upper management didn't speak French. Yet as a sales manager, she required adequate support from legal counsel, which she never got. Margaret was more disappointed than angry that she had no legal support moving forward to close the SLA deal. This was the first clash in which she learned she could not rely on Brad to provide adequate resource support. Unfortunately, she was only able to send the SLA two years later, after she developed a new service packet from the ground up for her Wallonia customer base. Faced with the lack of legal counsel and other challenges, the Wallonia region was subject to many decisions from Brad that failed to add value. No proper understanding of each department's responsibilities in the development and implementation of SLAs existed, nor did a contract administration plan with the participation and buy-in of other departments in the organisation. The contract administration was left with Margaret as the salesperson.

## The Salesperson Learns the Ins and Outs

During her first months on the job, Brad and Margaret hardly communicated with each other. Interaction between the two happened largely through emails. Although Margaret felt they would be necessary for smooth operation, there were no reviews of her region's business growth or monthly calls to discuss successes and challenges she experienced. After being denied such meetings, however, she accepted the situation. Margaret concluded that this was Brad's management style and she shouldn't worry. She knew he was very busy. Additionally, Margaret assumed Brad had enough confidence in her skills and capabilities that he believed she could do the job without much control and oversight from him. Knowing Margaret's region was in good hands, he must be devoting his attention to other sales regions given his additional role alongside that of CEO for Belgium: he was also EMEA sales director.

Like in many organisations, there were unhappy customers before Margaret began working for the Wallonia region. These customers had high expectations and were mainly dissatisfied with delayed project implementations, late product developments, and a lack of operational excellence.

Several new hires lacked the appropriate qualifications because they were taken on board out of nepotism and favouritism. These employees received critical roles within the organisation without having the right skills to perform their role successfully or experience working in a fast-paced environment. For instance, two years prior to Margaret's start date, the Wallonia office won a contract to install five hundred visual communication solutions. A new project manager got assigned to this top customer project. This was the beginning of potentially five thousand installations in total, a deal in the double-digit millions of euros. The potential installations were split into nine different deals for eighteen different regions in Wallonia. However, the assigned project manager was over-stressed by the complexity of the first five hundred installations, the customer's high demands, and the lack of guidance coming from Paul. The installations did not progress according to plan, and the product team was not advancing in the development of a compatible solution to increase the chances of winning the largest of the eight other deals, for one thousand installations. Naturally, the customer was unhappy with the organisation's overall performance. They had annual meetings with Brad, but the situation worsened. The customer wrote numerous complaint emails to Miriam, Paul, and Brad before Margaret came to work at the organisation.

It had been three years after winning this contract, and two months into Margaret's employment, when the unhappy customer sent their first complaint email to her, with Brad and Paul on copy. She translated the complaint email into English before sending it to Brad and Paul, along with her recommendation to consider assigning the stressed-out project manager to a different project where Margaret also needed help. They could assign a more experienced project manager who had just completed his previous project to this unhappy customer. Unfortunately, her recommendation was not implemented. Eighteen months later, the stressed-out project manager got discharged, and Brad hired an external consultant. This consultant was not hired to learn the products, people, processes, policies, or practices, but solely to manage the remaining one thousand installations, for which the organisation did not yet have a compatible solution.

At the time of the complaint email, Brad knew the stakes were high and the competition was close, but he still rejected Margaret's recommendation to select an internal project manager for this unhappy customer. She saw Brad's rejection as a failure to relate to the salesperson's perspective. This was the second clash of expectations, and she began to accept that she could not count on adequate resource support from Brad and Paul. Also, she began to realise that even though she had all the stress that came with meeting sales quotas and revenue targets, she had no decision authority whatsoever, and her opinion was weighted very low as a sales manager responsible for a sales region and the organisation's customers. Nonetheless, she knew the assigned project manager urgently needed help, since no other resources were allocated. So, over the following eighteen months, she supported the project manager in five thousand installation projects. During this eighteen-month period, she also had several commercial meetings with the customer in which she learned their four-year budget plan and that their top priority was to complete the installation of the five thousand solutions in the next two years. She and the overwhelmed project manager made as much progress on this goal as they could. This situation resulted in Margaret missing other business opportunities as she helped solve these project management challenges instead of solving Wallonia's business development challenges.

There came the only time Brad visited a customer with Margaret. Something Margaret keenly remembered about this day was when Brad revealed that his position as CEO for the Belgium office had been imposed upon him. She observed his weariness at this heavy burden and the frustration that would later lead him to prioritise his success as the EMEA sales director over his role as a CEO responsible for 110 employees in Belgium. Brad was a marketing manager before he got promoted to CEO, and Margaret assumed that Brad chose to have overall best KPIs as the EMEA sales director over meeting KPIs as the Belgium CEO. He wanted to show investors his best performance as a sales director, and one way he did this was by taking credit for work Margaret completed while simultaneously showing investors that Margaret's performance was unproductive. This was one of many ways in which Margaret realised Brad was selfish for success.

Faced with these and other challenges in her first months on the job, it took Margaret nearly a year to realise the extent of bias against the Wallonia region. She knew that Brad was either misinformed or unwilling to relate to her situation in terms of the resources she needed to do her job. She decided to develop a sales strategy with insights into the possible development of Wallonia's sales activities and lessons learned from past endeavours.

Margaret gathered business intelligence, then sent Brad a presentation addressing two key elements: (i) Her Wallonia sales strategy as a sales manager, and (ii) Wallonia's sales plan, with lessons learned which explained why revenues had been declining in the region before Margaret came to work with Brad.

**Sales strategy:** Margaret developed a sales strategy that addressed the following three topics:

1) Sales challenges (issues & concerns)
   - Wallonia Projects: The time currently spent on supporting projects resulted in significantly less time available to focus on the primary responsibility of business development to meet FY13 sales targets.
   - Responsibilities: Margaret was currently supporting various activities across multiple business areas such as project management, procurement, customer service, credit & collections, technical support, back-office operations, marketing, and contract management.
   - Pricing Strategy: Current price levels appeared uncompetitive, resulting in an increasing number of lost deals based on price (according to research and direct customer feedback).
   - Pricing Process: The ERP tool generated inaccurate pricing information, which contributed to the point above. The pricing processes as a whole needed to be reviewed and rectified to improve the chances of winning contracts.
   - Contracting Issues: Insufficient legal and contractual support were offered to ensure the

thorough review of all contracts to mitigate liability risks.

- Enterprise Documents: In Dutch and English only (i.e., not translated into French or German).

2) Recommendations (improvement measures)
- Wallonia Projects: Add a dedicated French-speaking technical representative with the right skill set to help capture additional SOW growth opportunities with existing customers.
- Responsibilities: Delegate tasks to additional French-speaking resources and increase focus on customer retention – a matter of business survival.
- Pricing Strategy: Develop a smart and comprehensive pricing strategy to ensure long-term success and profitability of the organisation with a cost-plus pricing model, a discount off-list price pricing model or competition-based pricing model. This would also improve the pricing approval process.
- Contracting Issues: Appoint legal counsel to ensure legal business rights are adequately protected and observed.
- Enterprise Documents: Add a translation office or additional French-speaking resources.

3) Benefits (outcomes)
- Wallonia Projects: The organisation will improve service delivery and operational excellence to create additional value over the competition.
- Responsibilities: A robust and healthy sales pipeline and improved sales forecast are ensured, along with the potential to overachieve fiscal year sales targets.
- Pricing Strategy: Improved bid positioning with more competitive pricing, along with transparency about actual profitability levels,

results in increased win ratios and a more profitable business.

- Pricing Process: The organisation will eliminate hidden costs and achieve quicker response time for receiving pricing – leading to higher conversion of leads and improved customer satisfaction.
- Contracting Issues: Improved commercial and contract management with robust service agreements results in reduced exposure to liabilities and penalties.
- Enterprise Documents: The organisation will maintain a consistent corporate identity, taking into account local and regional needs.

**Sales plan**: Margaret's approach and development of her sales plan for the first year included the following:

(1) Gathering insight on the region's top customers by archiving quality information Margaret acquired during customer meetings.

(2) Ensuring high-quality weekly and quarterly reporting.

(3) Implementing sales approaches calibrated to achieve her region's sales quotas.

In year two, she planned to focus on KPIs and improve customer satisfaction to build rapport with top customers and increase share of wallet (SOW) growth. Margaret would ensure customer complaints and their escalations were handled promptly. She would then identify flaws, examine best practices and lessons learned, and provide recommendations for improvement to implement in her region.

In year three, Margaret would position innovative solutions to fit market trends that all affiliated brands in the group were developing for the visual communication sector, including new service packages. The latter included a new managed services packet that Margaret would go on to develop from scratch.

## The Salesperson Assesses the Organisation

To achieve her goals in the first three months on the job, she built rapport with co-workers and asked questions to learn the way things worked within her organisation, its affiliated brands, and the group as a whole. She learned the organisation's ERP tool, although it was imperfect.

Her overall goal before beginning to interact with the customers in her region was to get as much business intelligence as possible about them.

She extracted customer history information from the ERP tool, identifying the following business intelligence to design her Wallonia sales strategy:

- Revenue figures from the past three years
- Revenue by product group
- Revenue by geography
- Group market share – The group, consisting of over a dozen affiliated brands, belonged to the portfolio of a large private equity firm, and each affiliated brand was located in a different country. It had an estimated overall European market share of around 30% and consisted of three business divisions:
    - The illuminated signage-element division accounted for 50% of the group's entire revenue.
    - The information and communications technology (ICT) division accounted for 25%.
    - The digital signage division accounted for 25%.
- EMEA revenue figures by sales territory and customer segment – After the acquisition, Brad became the new CEO for the affiliated brand in Belgium. His region accounted for less than 10% of the group's overall revenue. This affiliated brand's

overall revenue came from three different business models:

- o The original equipment manufacturer (OEM) customer base accounted for 45% of the organisation's total revenue.
- o Fortune 500 customers, large enterprise, and public-sector customers accounted for 40%.
- o Strategic alliances and partnerships accounted for 15%.

- The business intelligence Margaret gathered over a three-month period for the sales plan indicated that eight out of nearly one hundred total customers accounted for 80% of the Wallonia office's annual revenue. She learned what product segments sold better than others and which previous years achieved the best revenue growth and why. This provided some measure of the situation and gave her a sense of what her next annual sales target revenue would look like. Equipped with this information, she decided to build rapport with these top eight customers first. She didn't have the bandwidth to focus on relationships with the remaining middle to low-volume customers who accounted for 20% of revenue. In the first year, she visited each of the eight customers to get a better understanding of their challenges, concerns, goals, key decision-makers, and most importantly, their decision-making process. Also, she learned that about 50% of Wallonia's revenue came from standard off-the-shelf products and the other 50% came from products tailored for specific customer engineering projects. The sales process to develop a tailored product is more complex and long-lasting, which meant half of the region's revenue came in a resource-intensive way.

- Group strategy: In speaking to several other employees and customers, Margaret not only built rapport but gathered lessons learned and identified patterns which suggested why revenues continued to decline. One pattern that caught her attention was that the organisation in Belgium had a hard time delivering operational excellence to customers. She learned that there were no specific business models in place for their customers. For instance, the group managed OEM customers in the same way they managed Fortune 500 customers, large enterprise customers, public customers, and strategic alliances and partnerships. With more research, she saw that this was not only the case in Belgium but overall in the entire group. Margaret's assessment indicated that the group itself seemed to be missing strategies for their (i) business model, (ii) sales and product go-to-market process, and (iii) corporate culture.

Unfortunately, after she provided Brad with the business strategy and sales plan presentation, he didn't take note of her effort to gather business intelligence or the lessons learned, nor did he connect with Margaret's strategic sales approach and recommendations for the Wallonia office. The due diligence she exercised in carefully investigating, verifying, and analysing the data she obtained from the research went for nothing. There was no follow-up whatsoever from Brad. This was the third incident within ten months in which she felt Brad wasn't supportive of her approach on business development.

## The Boss Throws a Bone

After nearly fourteen months on the job, Brad approached Margaret with a promotion to the position of Belgium sales director. Delighted, Margaret thanked him for considering her for the role, but she wanted to know about additional benefits the job had to offer. Brad revealed that the sales director position didn't come with other benefits, nor would Margaret get a new contract. Given that information, she still felt it could be a great opportunity. To her, money was not everything. She accepted the challenge. After a few weeks on the job, Margaret sent Brad a sales plan for the Belgium market for his review. Naturally, her sales plan as the Belgium sales director differed from that of a sales manager for the Wallonia office.

The plan Margaret developed was first to solve the customers' pressing problems and then, as a continued sales action plan, to increase margin by (i) reducing the discount percentages offered or increasing selling price by 2-4%, (ii) cross-selling to higher-margin applications or to lower-cost applications, (iii) upselling to higher-priced components, (iv) attaching services, software, and other upsells, (v) no longer offering free items like connectors or cables, (vi) renegotiating existing price agreements and increasing selling prices, (vii) negotiating price agreements in order to maintain rich margins long term, and (viii) paying attention during product transitions to optimise the proposal and margins.

Unfortunately, none of these plans were able to be put into action because of how toxic this workplace turned out to be.

# Part II
# The Consequences of a Toxic Workplace

# Chapter 4

# Employee Disengagement

## Leadership Advice from an Innovator

Elon Musk is well-known as an innovator, visionary, and business owner.

He works to revolutionise transportation with Tesla, an electric vehicle and solar panel manufacturer. His interest in technology has also led him to start the Musk Foundation, dedicated to space exploration and the discovery of renewable, clean energy resources.

In terms of management theory, it appears that his approach in running a business is like managing a complex engineering project. In an email to his employees, Elon discussed their goals and provided some hints for productivity, along with his precise thoughts about management and corporate culture. It's worth examining these suggestions, taken from the email obtained by Electrek[3], to evaluate his challenges and how he hopes to solve them:

> *There is a very wide range of contractor performance, from excellent to worse than a drunken sloth. All contracting companies should consider the coming week to be a final opportunity to demonstrate excellence. Any that fail to meet the Tesla standard of excellence will have their contracts ended on Monday.*
>
> *Btw, here are a few productivity recommendations:*
> - *Excessive meetings are the blight of big companies and almost always get worse over time. Please get of all large meetings, unless you're certain they are*

---

[3]https://ww.electrek.co/2018/04/17/tesla-model-3-production-goal-6000-units-per-week/

*providing value to the whole audience, in which case keep them very short.*

- *Also get rid of frequent meetings, unless you are dealing with an extremely urgent matter. Meeting frequency should drop rapidly once the urgent matter is resolved.*

- *Walk out of a meeting or drop off a call as soon as it is obvious you aren't adding value. It is not rude to leave; it is rude to make someone stay and waste their time.*

- *Don't use acronyms or nonsense words for objects, software, or processes at Tesla. In general, anything that requires an explanation inhibits communication. We don't want people to have to memorize a glossary just to function at Tesla.*

- *Communication should travel via the shortest path necessary to get the job done, not through the "chain of command." Any manager who attempts to enforce chain of command communication will soon find themselves working elsewhere.*

- *A major source of issues is poor communication between depts. The way to solve this is to allow free flow of information between all levels. If, in order to get something done between depts, an individual contributor has to talk to their manager, who talks to a director, who talks to a VP, who talks to another VP, who talks to a director, who talks to a manager, who talks to someone doing the actual work, then super dumb things will happen. It must be ok for people to talk directly and just make the right thing happen.*

- *In general, always pick common sense as your guide. If following a "company rule" is obviously ridiculous in a particular situation, such that it would make for a great Dilbert cartoon, then the rule should change.*

When examining Elon's points, we can identify two groups of suggestions. The first three points can be interpreted as "keep meetings short and productive," and the last three points as "Strive for better communication." The last three are most relevant as they are vital for achieving a productive corporate culture and a healthy workplace, especially the requirement that "Communication should travel via the shortest path necessary to get the job done." Elon Musk's email does not only address the issue around communication, but it communicates that issue directly to Tesla's partners. Employees experience first-hand the manner of communication that Musk prefers. Many organisations have come to consider this point as one of their "Code of Conduct" principles. However, when we examine all of Elon's points together, we can identify one primary goal: "shortening the cycle of a specific activity." Since the world we live in is becoming ever more complex, the right mindset for leadership is to keep things as simple as they can be. This approach pays off. Today, in early 2020, the 49-year-old Elon Musk became the 34th-richest person in the world, and Tesla's market cap also hit $83 billion, making it the most valuable car company in American history according to data from Dow Jones[4].

While persistence is crucial for effective leadership, you should also be realistic and flexible. Effective leaders put things to the test, they learn from their lessons, and they calibrate their objectives. This means that they are prepared to pull out or change the plan's direction if they find that direction is not attainable. Effective leader like Elon Musk or Jeff Bezos would rather change their objective than chase one that is unachievable. Giving up a particular line of action does not mean that you are quitting. On the contrary, it means that you persist even as you challenge your initial assumptions and evaluate alternative ways of unique and sustainable value creation. Also, these leaders embrace the possibility that others might know better, and these leaders get out of their way if that helps moves progress forward. However, in less successful organisations than Tesla and Amazon, we still see leaders who are extremely self-assured: they think their

---

[4]https://www.barrons.com/articles/tesla-stock-most-valuable-car-company-51578415861

ideas and instincts are superior to anyone else's even when counterevidence has been presented.

## Signs of a Toxic Workplace for a Salesperson

It had now been nearly two years on the job, yet Margaret still spent about half of her time troubleshooting projects that were delayed, addressing damages done to these unhappy customers, and examining potential sources of growth to compensate for the deals missed while she was occupied as project management support over eighteen months. The situation was not improving and even posed a threat to the survival of the Wallonia office, but this merited no serious consideration from Brad. In fact, Brad was a source of many inefficiencies himself. In her weekly reports, Margaret had informed him of challenges such as:

- Sales engagement process: Margaret began to have difficulties coping with the heavy workload. She had no adequate product training, nor did she have presales support resources to help qualify the technical feasibility of an end-to-end solution. She was often dependent on other employees who knew the products better. However, they too had higher priorities. In Brad's international regions, meanwhile, technical representatives worked in close collaboration with salespeople on the technical drawing and configuration of end-to-end solutions in the presales phase. This engagement process got Margaret's attention, and she grew disappointed and concerned that a similar process didn't apply in her region, even though Brad knew this was necessary for them to perform best.
- Resource prioritisation: Margaret encountered conflicts of interest between international and regional business opportunities, which were in constant competition for limited resources. The prioritisation criteria were left for Brad and Paul to decide. Since Margaret's region was hardly a priority

to Brad, many business opportunities she qualified had to be scrapped because scarce resources were allocated to international opportunities or other activities instead. Margaret somewhat understood Brad and Paul's approach here – they wanted to steer resources to the opportunities they were most excited about – but the organisation could not afford to annoy customers, much less continue losing them at the current pace. Furthermore, Margaret didn't appreciate the fact that the entire leadership team lacked any action plan to mitigate these conflicts of interest and deblock the bottleneck of business opportunities so they would flow smoothly.

- Sales reporting, for instance, was cumbersome and time consuming because no CRM existed. Additionally, for unknown reasons, Brad required Margaret to send him an Excel sheet every Friday reporting on all her leads and possible conversion, plus those of all other sales regions. This repetitive work meant she could not plan customer meetings on Friday or she would risk not being able to send out the weekly sales activity report by noon, when Brad expected it. She didn't quite understand the logic of creating two files with the same content, especially since salespeople from other regions only filled in weekly sales reports once in OneNote. It was not an insignificant amount of work, either, but involved detailed descriptions and discussions to gather the information she would report. Nonetheless, Margaret ensured her reports included sales challenges, the business development activities she completed, deals she won, cost reductions activities she achieved in the presales phase, and comments on how many proposals she sent out that week. She hoped her reports would at least bring these achievements, opportunities, and areas of potential improvement to Brad's attention. All EMEA salespeople also had their regional challenges and mentioned these in their weekly reporting. However,

Margaret later realised that almost none of the negative reports over her three years at the company were ever followed up on by leadership. Nor did leadership ask questions or seek dialogue to understand the challenges she faced. Why even write about challenges if leaders don't act on them?

- Non-sales activities: Margaret had spent a lot of time assisting a project manager who lacked guidance and support from Paul, a lack that delayed the progress of many project installations. Because she was occupied with helping the project management team to address this problem, Margaret could not do the job she was hired to do, which was to develop business. In the short term, the organisation might have solved its project management challenges, but it wasn't solving its business development challenges because Margaret's abilities as a salesperson were underutilized for several months. Other non-sales tasks which Margaret had to deal with regularly were product lead time, order delivery delays, product quality issues, and delays in the post-sales project implementations phase – for instance, after the delivery of the goods, the installation often could not begin due to a missing component.

- Language barrier: This was another example of non-sales activities that consumed Margaret's time and the organisation's money. Much of her time was taken up by translating English or Dutch SLA contracts into French and developing product brochures and datasheets in French. Besides that, for nearly every French-speaking customer interaction, Margaret had to first translate the customer question before she could ask for support from any department in the organisation. Then, when feedback was provided, Margaret had to translate the answer back to French.

- The proposal submission process: There was no bid management team, and Margaret had to submit each French-language tender for any affiliated branded product by herself without an ERP solution that could develop complete end-to-end offers. Margaret asked Brad several times for support but to no avail. Only one affiliated brand agreed to submit French offers directly, and when they did this, the organisation optimised process management, improved productivity, increased the win probability, reduced overall EMEA costs, and improved process cycle time by avoiding repetitive work. This repetitive work, like when proposals for products from affiliated brands were submitted through Margaret, created estimated costs amounting to 15% of the selling price – and these were the savings achieved when the repetitive work was eliminated. This also created a better customer experience with quicker response and reaction time, from the offer submission to the order processing and finally to the delivery of the goods. When offers were submitted quickly, the organisation got the order faster, and this consequently shortened the sales cycle. However, Brad didn't connect to this approach. It seemed that in his view, if his international team did not have this success, no one else should, especially not Wallonia, even if that meant sacrificing his position as CEO for Antwerp – a job that he never wanted. Brad began to envy Margaret's success as he realised the health of the sales pipeline she had developed with other affiliated brands: she was winning new customer acquisition deals every four months, including deals for other affiliated brands of the group, and continued doing so for 36 months.

- Disregard for a single point of accountability: Margaret's region had qualified the most business opportunities for several different affiliated brands. To close these deals, Margaret had already established relationships with many of the affiliated brands' employees. Yet, since she had previously served as a single point of contact with her customer base in Wallonia, her customers were misled when a salesperson and other employees from a different affiliated brand visited them. These employees did not provide Margaret with any updates or meeting reports about their interactions with the customers in her sales region. Because many affiliated brands lacked a CRM tool, they isolated customer information and didn't pass it on to Margaret or other employees who needed to be informed about activities in their regions. Indeed, isolating information rather than sharing it was a known phenomenon in the group. Margaret, however, continued to keep communication going. After every customer visit, she shared relevant information, in the form of meeting reports, with specific employees and affiliated brands. She anticipated that others would soon begin to share important information after visiting customers in her sales region, too. Unfortunately, this did not come to pass.

- Employees practicing due diligence: It was essential to Margaret that a small region like hers, which lacked resource budgets, continued to keep their overhead costs low. At the same time, she wanted to identify potential areas to further optimise their sales resources, including the work of technical representatives and project managers. Since 40% of the presales work was done by a project manager, who was paid 15-30% more than a technical representative (TR), there was a great potential savings if this work could be completed instead by the lower-cost TR. On the contrary, however, Paul began to imagine a hybrid presales resource in which the project manager would be the same person as the TR. The hybrid approach was, in Margaret's view, destined to cause conflicts of interest because a project manager and technical representative have different competencies, knowledge, experience, responsibilities, and their deployment activities differ in the sales engagement process during the entire sales cycle. Many were unaware of Paul's decision-making criteria when, on behalf of Brad, he assigned product developer, project manager, and technical representative resources to business opportunities. Were his decisions based on what was strategically best for the organisation's product development strategy, or on what was best for Brad's favourite sales regions?

- The organisation's invoicing and credit & collections process brought Margaret additional challenges. For instance, one top customer who placed nine separate orders received over one hundred different invoices. Naturally, this annoyed the customer. Once again, due to the language barrier, Margaret had to play the intermediary between the customer's finance department and her organisation's credit & collections team. Solving this specific issue took nearly ten months.

- Budget allocation for new resources: During a conversation with Margaret, the organisation's finance director mentioned that her region had an allocated budget for new hires. Margaret was pleased to hear this, but she later found out that Brad had allocated this budget to his international team. A year later, more budget was approved to hire someone for Margaret's region. Again, she expected and hoped for the best, but Brad once more decided to allocate these resources to his international team. For the third year, a budget was allocated to hire two new employees for Margaret's region. These two new hires were located in the Wallonia office, but were instructed to work 70% of the time for Brad's international team. This lack of technical workforce was accompanied by a widespread lack of training from Paul's product development team. Not only that, but no action plan was in place for these technical employees to get training on products from other affiliated brands in the group.

- Lack of resources to meet customer needs: To continue meeting revenue goals, Margaret had to prioritize the eight customers who accounted for 80% of her region's sales revenue, and due to insufficient resources assigned to her region, she had to neglect the others.
- Problematic patterns leading to losses: When Margaret lost three software deals, she interviewed each of the three customers to identify the reasons they selected the competition over her organisation. She then sent a summary of these interviews to Brad and to the leaders of the affiliated brand who developed the software. Her goal was to evaluate possible action plans to mitigate future losses. In her interviews, Margaret learned several reasons why the competitor won, but three patterns stood out above the rest:
  - Customers had no confidence in the brand's software platform and were unwilling to take the risk.
  - Customers had never seen a live demonstration with a combination of both hardware and software.
  - Customers never received an evaluation unit, nor had they tested the brand's complete system themselves.

She sent the summary, and a few weeks later, an internal conference call took place where all involved stakeholders, including the software product development team, were present. During the conference call, one of the affiliated brand's product managers disagreed with the patterns Margaret identified from these customers. She told the product manager that this was direct customer feedback, and the identified patterns correlated with what Margaret and other salespeople had observed themselves. The product development team was certainly unhappy about this feedback, but the weakness in the software was widely known elsewhere in the organisation and they needed to hear about it directly from customers.

The sales plan Margaret sent to Brad when she became the new sales director for the Belgium market didn't get reviewed, nor did Brad provide feedback. Neither did he respond to address the challenges listed above, which she diligently mentioned in her weekly reports. After two years on the job as a sales manager for the Wallonia region, including six months as the Belgium sales director, Margaret still had no decision-making authority over Wallonia, let alone over the Belgium sales region. The problem within some organisations is that those who have innovative ideas have no power to enforce them, and those with power have no innovative ideas.

Though Margaret's region won over a dozen deals worth double-digit millions of euros, and she built a sales pipeline worth double-digit millions, in the same thirty-month period her region also lost many deals worth single-digit millions. There were also concerns about the ability to serve existing clients. In order to handle these challenges and to avoid further losses in the Wallonia region, Margaret finally decided to call up Brad and inform him of her decision to resign from her Belgium sales director position but remain on as a sales manager.

After the phone conversation, she sent the following email to Brad:

*Dear Brad,*

*I herewith inform you that I will resign as the sales director for the Belgium market effective September 1st. I will keep my role as a sales manager for the Wallonia office.*

*I appreciated being considered for the sales director role, but based on the current circumstances described below, stepping down is, in my opinion, the best option:*

> *The healthy revenue and margin growth in the Wallonia office need my full capacity and*

*attention. Therefore, and because of the point discussed below, I believe I can serve you and the organisation better as a sales manager for the Wallonia office rather than in the Belgium sales director role.*

➢ *The sales director promotion is a promotion only on paper. There is additional workload but no adequate resources are provided. The promotion gave me a better title, but no benefits or improvement in conditions.*

➢ *The French and German language barriers the organisation faces in different departments requires a great deal of my time to manage. On top of that, the demands of my duties as a sales director (e.g., extra work, more responsibilities, managing people, balancing a bigger budget without additional resources) are affecting my health. In light of these factors, it seems as though the promotion comes with unrealistic performance expectations.*

➢ *The sales manager role is captivating, and my reputation as a sales specialist is beneficial for the Wallonia office and the organisation throughout Belgium.*

*I hope for your understanding.*
*Sincerely,*
*Margaret*

## A Narcissistic Leadership Style Creates Ostracism

People are very aware of when they are being labelled or excluded at work, whether from communication or a decision-making process, or when they find themselves being shunned by co-workers socially. Workplace ostracism does great harm to employee happiness. This leads to unproductive and uncreative behaviour, not least because of the toll it takes on employees' wellbeing. Such behaviour is one of the major causes of disengagement in the workforce.

To a certain degree, everyone is biased, and nearly everyone subconsciously labels people and situations according to stereotypes. Though an exclusionary or biased behaviour is subconscious, that doesn't make it less disturbing.

On the other hand, creating a work environment where employees feel included is directly connected to retention and growth. Real leadership is about modelling transparency and openness. The best leaders understand themselves and value others' input, making this clear to everyone around them. When leaders create inclusion, the business benefits are profound. Employees who feel included and appreciated are productive. They deliver better results and become loyal and trustworthy. Inclusion can attach an employee to a cause morally and emotionally, resulting in a stronger work ethic. That is why a leader's behaviour and communication style have the most significant impact on corporate culture. Leaders should always foster environments where employees, regardless of age, race, gender, or personality type, feel valued.

The narcissistic leadership style allows and creates deviant behaviour, which threatens the overall wellbeing of employees and the development of a healthy workplace. These leaders intend to intimidate, and they may also be motivated to disparage others' behaviour. They are also predisposed to engage in practices that ultimately harm the organisation and its members. Narcissists are hyper-vigilant to perceived threats, and when their self-concept is threatened, they are likely to engage in aggressive behaviour. Narcissistic behaviour by leaders (i.e. self-absorption, grandiosity and arrogance, hostility, and fragile self-esteem) is related to higher levels of ostracism, even if that leader has high behavioural integrity for the organisation's intended outcome.

When employees trust their leaders, they perform better; they display greater commitment that results in higher job satisfaction, which also means they are less likely to leave the organisation. Narcissistic leaders, on the other hand, create an atmosphere of suspicion that erodes the organisation's health at all levels. Even when employees continue to show integrity, the benefits of their good behaviour and due diligence are neutralised by the leader's toxic personality and poor behaviour. An organisation's lack of success can be often linked to an atmosphere in which leaders are not held accountable and where a power struggle exists.

Corporate culture is not as easy as just hiring the right people, nor as simple as handing out a new induction training handbook, but it's somewhat common-sense ethics. It's created by the motivation and ability to understand and live a value system as individuals, teams, and an organisation as a whole. Yet no matter what industry you work in or whom you hire, all people can be corrupted, and without control over your corporate culture, this happens more often than you might expect.

# Chapter 5

# Leaders' Bad Character and Behaviour

The general outline of charismatic leadership goes:
(i)   The strategic, transformational leader has a vision for the organisation.
(ii)  He inspires people to make sacrifices for the good of the organisation, in line with its vision and mission statement.
(iii) Additionally, he empowers people to work towards accomplishing the vision and mission statement.

Charisma by itself, however, does not guarantee a leader's effectiveness. The key innovation in the growing corporate culture approach has been the reduction of charismatic leadership to the formula and reliance on other traits. Some experts place more emphasis on the moral qualities of a leader. Others focus on commitment, and yet others place more emphasis on one's EQ (emotional intelligence, or emotional quotient) than one's IQ (intelligence quotient).

## Flawed Assumptions

As Margaret assessed the organisation's situation, she realised it now consisted of nearly one thousand employees worldwide who had not yet experienced any type of internal organisational change management pre- or post-M&A. Consequently, all leaders of these colliding cultures and brands, now belonging to a single group, were working hard to keep business moving as usual for their brand, rather than the dozen affiliated companies working together to build a business strategy for the entire group, which is usually the intended end in mind of a M&A.

The lack of organisational change management after the M&A resulted not only in a lack of efficiency but in a chilling workplace culture, overrun by doublespeak and defamation of character. A book comes to mind called *Doublespeak*. The author, William D. Lutz, writes about how government, businesses, advertisers, and others use language to deceive us. His conclusion: throughout time, language has progressively evolved, and so have the methods used to manipulate the views of the people. Doublespeak represents a danger to society because of how it influences our actions and thoughts. It distorts reality by creating false communications based on contradiction, misleading words and phrases, and unnecessary complexities.

When examining the entire situation, it seemed that due to unknown factors, possibly fear, Brad wanted Margaret's region to fail. He continued to make non-value-added decisions which all but ensured that Margaret's region became a high-cost centre, unprofitable, and a toxic workplace for a salesperson to try to succeed in. Furthermore, Brad began involving teams and individuals in ways that disrupted operations. For instance, a group of four employees from Brad's brand would visit customers in Margaret's region without informing or engaging her as the responsible salesperson for that region. This team didn't evaluate or understand the negative consequences this could have for the organisation's brand and to the limited number of customers in Margaret's sales region. At one point, Margaret addressed this concern with Brad during a meeting, but her concerns were ignored.

The internal power struggle between EMEA's leaders was another significant issue that led to high employee turnover. This was exacerbated by mergers and acquisitions, which meant the group now included four formerly competing brands. The aftermath of M&A always impacts employees, and leaders rarely welcome organisational change management after one because they're worried about their jobs. The fear factors throughout the affiliated brands were high, and due to Brad's lack of commitment towards helping

Margaret's region succeed – he focused far more on opportunities in other EMEA sales regions, even though the Wallonia office was also his responsibility – a follow-up with him was futile. Brad's tampering with her region's business progress, including the way he prevented disclosure of weekly sales reports, had done more bad than good not only for Wallonia but also for Belgium as a whole.

Over many years, Brad created a very toxic, biased environment for any salesperson to stay in. Margaret identified these patterns in her first ten months on the sales job and concluded that once Brad had forced her predecessor, Miriam, to leave a few years before her retirement, Margaret was hired to continue Miriam's struggle with him. She learned her region was not a priority for Brad. Indeed, her region's business progress was being hindered; resources were allocated to other areas, business growth was being blocked, and her weekly reports were altered before being sent to the EMEA leadership team and headquarters (HQ) in the US.

By accident, Margaret was able to see that her sales reports for a specific week were missing from the summary table sent to the EMEA leadership team and HQ. This meant it was likely that during the entire period of her employment, Brad had enhanced or removed information from Margaret's reports before he sent the summary to the EMEA leadership team and HQ. In short, Brad committed defamation of Margaret's character in the workplace, and his tampering with her reports may also constitute unprivileged publication and evidence of libel. For instance, by removing Margaret's entire weekly sales activity content, Brad implied to investors that her weekly sales performance activities were unproductive. His misrepresentation of her accomplishments injured Margaret's reputation, and her work was already made difficult because of workplace ostracism. Individual departments shunned her and withheld the resources Margaret required in the presales phase. Brad, Rachael, Paul, and other co-workers knew the resources she needed to succeed were being blocked from her, but no one acted. Margaret addressed Brad about this resource-blocking, the bias against her, and constant dispute with co-workers in the Wallonia office and informed him that she would work remotely until the issue was examined. She did her due diligence by addressing this concern to Brad, but he didn't take her complaint seriously, nor did he attempt to investigate what she had experienced with co-workers in the Wallonia office. Even after the truth came out about this bias and ostracism against Margaret, Brad still didn't take proper action. Nor did anyone else, although many employees knew about the blocking of resources, the employee disengagement in her region, and the toxicity due to insults that came from co-workers. Too often, in these large workplace crowds, the bystander effect and diffusion of responsibility manifest, making such misconduct possible.

Brad never related to Margaret's point of view or the recommendations in her weekly sales reporting activities, yet he still took credit for work Margaret did. As someone coming from the outside and who had worked with different organisation types, she was able to suggest best practices that had turned out well for other brands. Besides, Margaret knew her customers better than Brad could have. She was perfectly positioned to add value to the organisation. Her insights would have addressed and solved many of the challenges it faced. The revenue decline in Margaret's region had made it clear that the current sales approach, used over many years, was costly and inefficient. Furthermore, the technical representative engagement process was carelessly designed and initiated in the presales phase because it had been developed by a project manager for project management instead of being developed in collaboration with the sales team with a goal of shortening the sales cycle.

Apart from the deals lost to local and EU competitors, postponements of customer projects, or changes in customer demands, Margaret identified several patterns behind why revenue declined. These included the following:

- Delayed project implementations due to unrealistic plans and poor resourcing decisions.

- Challenges in the sales engagement process, particularly the lack of presales and back-office support. Furthermore, technical representatives didn't engage early in the sales cycle. Instead, they only engaged when customer orders came in-house.
- Lack of experience or training of new hires in best-practice methods (e.g. communication with all stakeholders, creating a risk response team, holding project kick-off meetings, using detailed work definition documents, creating a comprehensive sales plan, documenting and archiving everything, asking for feedback, identifying new service packages for SLAs, holding short and efficient wrap-up meetings).

The evidence showed that the current sales approach had cracks and badly needed a re-evaluation. These cracks ended up being catastrophic for the revenue in Margaret's region because they hindered innovative advancements and occupied salespeople with non-sales activities. Where best-practice sales methods aren't incorporated into operations, salespeople won't be able to do their jobs efficiently.

Using Margaret's experience as a case study, the following are some characteristics that tend to foreshadow a toxic workplace:

- An internal power struggle among the leadership.
- An autocratic leadership/management style, often combined with a lack of internal communication from leadership.
- Reporting policies that further dilute accountability.
- Poor employee engagement, including lack of enthusiasm and lack of knowledge or cooperation among co-workers.
- Exclusion of employees outside the dominant zone (whether in terms of cultural background, race, gender, or other identities), who aren't shown hospitality during their entrance into the organisation or throughout their employment. Communication skills of those in the dominant zone need improvement with the different teams and groups, as many are left

out of the loop, which affects how matters are dealt with or responded to.

- Pressure to meet short-term goals, especially when this comes without the assignment of adequate success factors to achieve these goals.
- An environment where employees are discouraged or afraid to speak up, leading to stagnation and apathy. No action is taken to address evidence that workers have been victimised as a result of speaking up.
- Defamation (libel and slander) and ostracism in the workplace. This can include the spreading of rumours, unprivileged publication, misrepresentation, gossip, or being shunned by co-workers, groups, and leaders, all of which can take a significant toll on the targeted employee's health and wellbeing.

## Competitive Advantage Through an Effective Business Model

After working for the organisation for over two years, Margaret, who had prior experience working in vertical market industries while using different business models, was confident that her organisation needed to re-evaluate the economic sustainability of its existing business model. But how could she motivate leadership to take action if they hadn't already noticed the business model challenge over many years and after so many M&As?

Paul knew Margaret had experienced several product transitions over her professional sales career, and he was open to suggestions since he had little to no experience in product transition strategies or product lifecycle management (PLM). Indeed, he was happy for guidance. Margaret had a great deal of empathy and shared her insights to help the organisation improve product transitions and PLM. For over a year, she and Paul had weekly meetings to discuss these topics. During a one-hour conference call for a brainstorming session, the two agreed that EMEA needed to isolate the product innovation development team or re-evaluate the organisation's business model. They also agreed that EMEA product innovation could not be led mainly by customer projects. During the call, Margaret explained the different customer requirements for each market segment to Paul. For instance, the public-sector customers and those from large enterprises needed product stability and the capacity of the organisation to perform business activities in that market segment.

Meanwhile, Fortune 500 customers and those from the OEM market segment additionally required:

- Global product pricing
- Product standardisation
- PLM/Product transitions

Paul gathered knowledge on product transition strategies and how to improve the organisation's PLM, at the same time shortening product time to market. Like Brad, Paul took all the credit for the work Margaret prepared.

Later Margaret learned that, rather than examining the economic sustainability of the existing business model, the organisation's leadership decided to isolate two business units, the product innovation and project teams, while letting everything else remain the same. The leadership's plans involved no specific market segmentation approach for their Fortune 500, OEM, large enterprise, and public-sector customers, nor for their strategic alliances and partnerships. It had become clear that she and the leaders of the organisation were not on the same page.

How an organisation provides its customers with more value than its competitors, and profits from that, is its business model. It includes the values provided to each market segment, a product or service for the market segment, activities for providing that product and/or service, and sufficient resources and competency to perform business activities in specific sectors. The business model is also a factor that can lead to declining performance in the organisation's bottom line. Challenges presented by the constant disruption from technology and innovation make organisations' business models more vulnerable in today's environment than ever. These changing market trends influence both an organisation's strategy and its business model. With Industry 4.0 on the horizon, companies need to ask themselves whether their existing model is still economically sustainable.

The Internet has created opportunities for businesses to preserve margins from traditional growth strategies by maintaining expense levels and using the resources it offers for product innovation, branding, and marketing communications. These factors don't counterbalance the forces moving commoditisation, and consequently, price competition because:

- The number of organisations providing goods and services enables any company to reproduce another company's product or service, turning even high-end product offerings and technologies that are new on the market into commodities.

- The Internet has reduced entry point barriers, meaning that organisations have more new competitors from across the world. Globalisation has caused the supply of products to grow relative to the demand for them, further intensifying competition.

- The Internet and mobile technology have also created greater price transparency. Customers can more easily compare prices than ever before.

- Customers have control today over when and how they are exposed to an organisation's message, through advertising or other means. They are more likely to create their impressions based on sources a company cannot control, such as reviews or complaints on social media.

- Apart from the internet factors, another modern opportunity and threat comes from GPOs. A group purchasing organisation (GPO) leverages the purchasing power of a group of businesses to obtain discounts from vendors based on the collective buying power of the GPO members. There are many benefits for businesses to joining a purchasing group, such as lower cost of goods purchased from vendors, lower shipping costs, centralised ordering, and support from the GPO itself. To vendors, however, they can represent a loss of profit due to the discounts involved.

Almost all business models eventually become obsolete. In response, organisations need to adapt their business models to external threats and opportunities. An organisation's business model may also become the basis of a competitive advantage, which is then a complementary element to the product features, benefits, and value it delivers to its customers. Innovation is about bringing value, but out of euphoria or uncertainty, many organisations lose interest in innovating their business models. They overlook this vital opportunity to gain a competitive advantage and capture new markets. It's a shame, because business models have generally proven vital to capture opportunities in new markets and improve the bottom line.

Successful organisations actively and consistently consider and pursue new business model strategies. Indeed, developing a well-differentiated business model is another way for companies to protect their margins. Periodic re-evaluation also helps leaders question their previous assumptions and make better decisions for business continuity and growth.

Successful business model execution focuses on designing a culture and process so that the organisation consistently delivers on its value promises, while keeping those promises unique to create a hard advantage that others simply cannot reproduce. The design and implementation of the internal engagement process for better customer experience is a critical part of this work. Changes to any part of the model can be proactive or forced by innovation or competitors. Effective leaders establish operating practices and a strong understanding of market conditions to evolve their business model as the world around them changes. Smart leadership teams recognise that different kinds of leaders are best positioned to lead different types of change.

## Weighing and Rating Priorities

When innovation development resources are prioritised for specific customer projects, this can damage the long-term recurring revenue of your standard product portfolio. This is especially true when only half of your revenue comes from standard products being sold, and the remaining half comes from customer projects, as in Margaret's employer's case. Six months into the job, she had learned that most of the organisation's product development resources were being used to innovate new products, features, and functions for customer-specific projects, meaning fewer resources were used for standard product lifecycle management. As a result, to grow the sales pipeline, the EMEA salespeople had no other choice than to position products that were in the pipeline but did not yet exist and might never be developed.

If the product development department fails at long-term innovation, salespeople shouldn't be the ones to blame for not delivering positive revenue results. Salespeople are not in the product management department, nor are they in the HR department, the project department, or the finance department. If the sales revenue numbers don't add up at the end of the financial year, it will be blamed on salespeople and no one else. This would be the case even when product time to market played a vital role, or the project management team couldn't progress with the completion of a project rollout.

In Margaret's organisation, product innovation was handled faultily. The salespeople realised that Paul had difficulty with his role as CTO (Chief Technology Officer) because of his lack of experience. He had never led the technology or engineering department nor worked as a product manager, thus he had no knowledge of best-practice methods. Product innovation should be aligned to overall organisational strategy, not to specific customer projects, whose narrow application can be a distraction. Along with issues around product roadmaps, product transition strategies, and product lifecycle management, this was also apparent in the failure to implement individual, department-specific training programs and materials. Nor was there continued follow-through on hardware and software training. The organisation failed to recognise or avoided acknowledging these challenges, and this impacted the training for employees within the entire group.

Rather than working with Paul on innovation, Brad took it upon himself to dictate when product development for a customer project began and when a product reached end-of-life (EOL). The approach Brad took might have worked several years before, but now that they had been in a group of affiliated branded companies for nearly four years, it badly needed recalibration.

## How Does Your Organisation Prioritise Innovation?

Innovation can be a frightening idea for those who don't work in this space. Innovation changes the way things are done, as well as confronting the uncertainty of how to deliver value. Achieving the right balance depends on several internal and external factors and a carefully managed process. Innovation in both product development and business optimisation can be divided into different phases. Each phase has several milestones. Only after each milestone is complete will the next step begin. This step-by-step approach leads to better control of time, money, and quality, and to successful product launches.

To consider the context of innovation in your business optimisation process, think about aspects like:

- How is innovation led in your organisation today?
- What are the set boundaries (what exactly are you attempting to solve, what types of response are you seeking, and which seem satisfactory)?
- Who is involved in enhancing innovation?
- What, if any, are the organisational implications of this innovation?

- What is the health of your workplace like, and how will that impact business innovation for better or worse?

The internal and external factors for innovation in product development are similar to those involved in business optimisation, with a few additional aspects such as:

- Lessons learned from successful and unsuccessful experiences.
- Direct customer feedback.
- Insights and trends suggesting where your market is heading.
- What the "www" (world wide web) says about your organisation – how are your products reviewed and recommended on ecommerce websites, blogs, or social media?
- Competitor analysis.
- Which of the three goal-driven approaches the organisation gives its product teams when developing a new product:
  1) Problem -> they provide the product management team information about the problem at hand and tell them to find a solution to solve this problem.
  2) Solution -> they tell the product management team, "This is the solution we want. Build it."
  3) Metric -> they provide the product team with metrics to achieve within a given timeline, such as product features, functions, development costs, or proper dimensions (e.g., weight, height, and length) and leave them to develop a product that fits these metrics.

People don't really like change, and innovation can signal discomfort and uncertainty to many. This is when your corporate culture should kick in to welcome transformation.

# Chapter 6

# Due Diligence in Mergers & Acquisitions (M&A)

## Change Management Pre- and Post-Mergers & Acquisitions

When it comes to M&A arrangements such as the one that consolidated the twelve affiliated brands of the group Margaret worked for, the winners are usually PE firms, and not necessary their investors. PE firms buy a company and leverage it for three to five years. However, the investment funds which these firms set up usually run for ten-year periods. At the point at which the company is sold, the contract that runs for ten years has to be bought out. Let's say the company is sold at the end of five years. Therefore, the PE firm will be paid, by the organisation they acquired, for an additional five years of services that they will not provide because they no longer own the company. The trick with PE firms is that it's not the PE firm borrowing money from investors, it's technically the company they are buying that borrows the money. PE firms collect excessive fees from the companies they own and fail to share these fees with the investors in their funds, who might have no knowledge of the existing ten-year contracts.

Many of the affiliated brands in Margaret's group entered the visual communication sector in the early 1980s and went on to become well-established brands in the late 1990s. However, in the mid-2000s, many affiliated brands' values deteriorated, to the point that some faced insolvency or bankruptcy. This finally led to the M&A by the PE firm. However, rather than uniting forces towards building a business strategy for the group, the now dozen affiliated brands, especially the four that used to be competitors, continued their competitive power struggle. The lack of leadership collaboration and the poor investor involvement and governance resulted in each affiliated brand representing itself just as it had before the M&A. The long-term goal of an M&A is usually that when two companies unite, one company ceases to exist after becoming absorbed by the other, precisely to avoid such conflicts.

When an organisation is acquired or when companies merge, the decision is typically based on a product or market fit, while colliding brand affection and employee cultures are often ignored. Human organisations are influenced by human behaviour and therefore cannot be simply added together by the numbers. A bicultural audit diagnosing cultural relations between the two merging organisations is necessary to minimise the cultural collision that occur in M&A.

It's a big mistake to assume that employee issues are easy to overcome, and CEOs that fail to recognise these end up regretting it. Then, when leaders realise some employees encounter difficulties because of these brand affection and culture challenges, rather than relating to their situation and offering encouragement, too often the leaders instead choose to terminate the employees' contracts. Worse yet, some leaders may even begin with defamation in the workplace; they dismiss or write off employees and make non-value-added decisions for their department or sales regions, as in Margaret's case. Rather than being terminated, the targeted employees may finally decide to leave the organisation themselves. This establishes a toxic work environment that leads to high employee turnover or employee burnout.

Is the saying true, then, that employees leave managers, not companies? In my opinion, the answer is yes. People leave bad managers. A leader who is unable or unwilling to relate to an employee's situation or work towards addressing their concerns will have difficulty retaining employees in the long run.

Communication challenges, meanwhile, are the number one reason that M&A synergies fail. Communication with employees, empowering them, and creating a culture for them to thrive are all fundamental parts of a transformation integration practice.

When a M&A occurs, employees are generally left in the dark. Rumours fill the vacuum, and employees are left asking questions like: Why is the organisation merging? How will the merger affect my work? What support will I receive during the merger process? In answer, they have only mysteries. This lack of communication creates distrust and leads to lower employee engagement throughout the workplace. Whenever there is a M&A, the new organisation attempts to downsize, resulting in business efficiency where it now requires a smaller number of people to perform the same task. Departing employees may benefit from the layoff as they move onto greener pastures, but this still has an impact on morale. Furthermore, at least some dedicated, motivated employees need to remain with the organisation to continue its work and preserve knowledge and continuity, as discussed a little later. The impact a M&A has on leaders may involve dents to their pride when they are asked to implement policies or strategies under the new organisation's HQ. As a result, the organisation's focus gets diverted, and leaders become busy with an internal power struggle when settling matters among themselves. However, leaders equipped with sufficient qualification and motivation to migrate to another company may not be troublesome at all.

Communication is a skill that ideally should come naturally. However, it can be the hardest skill to learn. When leaders fear conflict, they tend to break down the communication lines that run throughout the organisation.

A survey conducted by Harris Poll on behalf of Interact[5] revealed that a majority (69%) of leaders confess to being uncomfortable communicating with their staff. This discomfort shows up in various ways, from ignoring the real issues to being unavailable or relying on email for

---

[5]http://interactauthentically.com/new-interact-report-many-leaders-shrink-from-straight-talk-with-employees/

communication. Leaders and employees can only be sure of effective communication when they observe an individual's behaviour after communicating with them. If an individual's behaviour does not change according to what was said, the leader or employee knows their communication is just an illusion.

When managing any key project, such as M&As, it's important to keep the employees from both parties informed at all times. Employees should learn about the progress of the integration through different communication channels such as email and internal newsletters. Leadership should be aware of questions, concerns, and fears that employees may have and proactively communicate answers to help build transparency and trust. All these factors together will lead to a successful merger.

Employee retention during M&A is challenging, and many leaders are concerned about the threat of losing a significant percentage of the workforce. Retention issues often result from negative attitudes felt by employees. These can include uncertainty about the organisation's future direction or the employee's job security, scepticism or concern about leadership credibility, and confusion due to lack of communication. In essence, employees may want to leave because they lose trust in their organisation and feel betrayed by their leadership. During this delicate process, however, it's essential to keep employee turnover low because business continuity is key to realising the benefits of the M&A. There can also be large financial implications from the cost of hiring new employees, which both incurs training expenses and results in loss of knowledge and customer relationships.

The loss of employees during the M&A process inevitably affects daily business activities. This has a hierarchical chain reaction – in that the employees who are the best and most committed to the previous state of the organisation may be the first to leave – which risks further demoralisation of an already compromised workforce. Companies envisioning M&As should focus not only on retaining key executives for the long haul but also on keeping faith with employees who show good to great KPIs. Failing to keep a critical mass of the old guard could set off a domino effect that the organisation will feel for many years to come. When M&As occur because the financial and business rationale adds up, too often leaders fail to realise the cultural risks. Along with the costs of employee turnover, these can result in missed business opportunities, low productivity, or even, in the worst cases, harmful brand exposure and devastating lawsuits when conflicts erupt and former employees leave with actionable claims against the workplace.

The people aspect of any M&A is always critical. Companies must proactively listen to employees to regain their trust, keep them with the company, and utilise the intellectual asset they represent. Reduction and replacement strategies also play a crucial role in the integration during M&A.

During the merger, it's easy to treat a prospective transaction as purely mechanical and a scientific process. However, it's difficult for a merged organisation to take on the culture of the merging organisation quickly because employees seldom replace their values and beliefs all at once. Generally, when M&As occur, they bring shifts in leadership principles, practices, and strategies that will have a range of implications for the people in the organisation. A sudden shift of these practices brings disruption and unease.

Appropriate due diligence before the merger will identify potential issues to address. It's also vital to conduct culture surveys to determine the norms within both organisations. Cultural influence has the potential to be broad and far-reaching. For example, decision-making at one organisation can be different from that of the other organisation, even its polar opposite. The leadership's social style could be dictatorial or consultative, and the way people work could be formal or based on informal relationships. For whatever reason an M&A occurs, the decision-makers must take these intangible factors into account.

It's difficult to relate or quantify the human side to mergers, and so they are often overlooked. Often CEOs are not concerned about this aspect because they have the notion that they can always hire new employees and leaders. However, in the long term, this creates detrimental outcomes. Remaining employees feel unvalued, and the merged organisation resists as it feels itself being swallowed and disappearing as an organisation.

For CEOs, executives, and leaders to fully understand the extent to which the merger will affect the culture, they should develop a culture strategy. Any tool may be appropriate so long as it measures overall cultural values, habits, and skills within the organisation. Through continuous feedback, leaders are able to understand their employees' concerns and issues before they become a threat to the organisation in the long run. By implementing such a strategy, the merging organisation can understand where the cultural differences are, engage with employees throughout the merging period, and carry out a successful culture shift.

## Strategy Against Brand and Culture Collision During Mergers & Acquisitions

After Dell and EMC[6] joined forces, survey scores for employee satisfaction were high. This is a rare accomplishment and a testament to the power of transparency and listening to employees. Merging companies creates uncertainty, fear, and tension among employees. Colliding cultures are the top reason why M&As often fail to achieve their promised growth value. When Dell and EMC came together in September 2016 to become the world's largest privately controlled information technology company, Dell Technologies, the aim was to ensure a smooth transition for their combined workforce of 138,000 employees. According to a November 2016 Tell Dell internal

---

[6]http://i.dell.com/sites/doccontent/corporate/corp-comm/en/Documents/fy17-cr-report.pdf

survey, 82% of team members felt inspired. Despite the ongoing integration of the teams, 81% of those surveyed already felt like they were part of the Dell team.

A vital element to Dell's success lies in its transparent, consistent communication and culture integration. Dell sought to develop a culture code that drives how they run the business, go to market, effectively interact with others, and provide inspirational leadership. As part of developing the culture code, Dell surveyed more than 75,000 Dell and EMC team members on the cultural attributes they believed would be most important to the success of their new organisation. A culture task force of both Dell and EMC employees then analysed the results and found not only that the two organisations' cultures were very much the same, but both qualified the same top cultural attributes, in the same order.

In addition to Dell Technologies' values, their culture code outlines seven leadership principles: relationships, drive, judgment, vision, optimism, humility, and selflessness. Dell Technologies rolled out their culture code and leadership principles globally by incorporating them into the ecosystem of all culture and talent practices.

To measure team members' acceptance of the code during the integration process, and to address concerns and queries, an internal communications team hosted weekly question and answer segments on their intranet. Dell Technologies also developed a clear line of communication from the Chief Integration Officer through a network of more than 2,000 integration ambassadors. The leadership frequently shared updates with ambassadors, who then dispatched insights to their teams. The ambassadors' goal was to help leaders understand team members' common concerns, which they did by using an internal social media tool (Salesforce Chatter) to interact with their fellow employees and collect questions and feedback about topics such as benefits and sales quotas.

In itself, the integration was a culture-building design exercise, said Dell Director of Global Employment Brand Jennifer Newbill. "Our work was so collaborative. By the time we reached Day One, it felt like our Dell and EMC teams had been working together for years." The integration teams continued to survey team members, respond to queries, and provide a transparent, open line of communication through FY18.

These are the shared values of Dell Technologies' culture code, the Code of Conduct titled "How We Win":

1. Customer: We believe our customer relationships are the ultimate differentiator and the foundation for our success.
2. Winning Together: We believe in and value our people. We perform better, are smarter, and have more fun working as a team than as individuals.
3. Innovation: We believe our ability to innovate and cultivate breakthrough thinking is an engine for growth, success, and progress.
4. Results: We believe in being accountable to an exceptional standard of excellence and performance.
5. Integrity: We believe integrity must always govern our fierce desire to win.

## Code of Conduct

Ethical business is a matter of obligation to comply with the law and adhere to an organisation's principles, policies, and standards at all times. In this way, employees exercise good consciousness of the organisation's assets, the environment, and how to perform their job safely and ethically. When employees' behaviour towards each other is not guided by a code of conduct, the result is often subpar or even abnormal functioning of an organisation.

Creating, following, and maintaining the code of conduct is both an individual responsibility and collective one. Organisations require a central guide and reference to support employees' day-to-day decision-making. A formal code of conduct encourages compliance, and it empowers employees to reflect on ethical dilemmas they encounter in the workplace.

A formal code of conduct often makes sense for organisations with over twenty employees. However, even small organisations may be significantly impacted by ethical issues. For instance, unprivileged publication and communications about a co-worker can constitute defamation in the workplace no matter its size – or think about a romantic relationship in the workplace that may lead to a sexual harassment lawsuit.

Leaders must ensure they support the code; they should coach their teams to enforce compliance and practice due diligence by conducting investigations and overseeing the appropriate consequences, following the directives of legal counsel where necessary. Leadership, human resources, and other employees must ensure confidentiality as part of standard due diligence procedures, at the same time encouraging everyone in the organisation to report concerns about a possible code of conduct violation through any available channels. The failure of employees to report a code breach, or to alert management that one is likely to occur, may result in criminal or financial penalties or damage to an organisation's reputation.

The code of conduct is a summary of complex ethical and legal guidelines to help employees understand basic rules that apply – and every employee's responsibility is to comply. It has value as both an internal guideline and as a visible statement of the organisation's committed values.

# Chapter 7

## Accountability and Reporting Policies

### The Point of No Return

As Margaret began her third year with the organisation, the situation was going from bad to worse. Alongside Brad's failure to support Margaret and the Wallonia office, he constructed policies and processes in multiple departments that delayed progress. At some point, the bar for employee expectations was raised very high, beyond possibility given these counterproductive practices, and Margaret found it very difficult to manage the stress of the situation. After nearly thirty months of struggling, she had no choice but to blow the whistle. The evidence she had obtained over the years on Brad's misconduct was overwhelming, and she sought counsel from the HR department.

By coincidence, this was when a new head of human resources, Elias, was hired in the Antwerp office for the group. Margaret thought that as the new HR leader, Elias would be the right person to speak to about Brad's wrongdoing. The first time the two of them spoke was at a company outing once Elias had been with the organisation for about four months. Margaret brought up the topic of the code of conduct the organisation lacked. Elias hinted that this was his priority because he knew without one, the organisation was open to legal liability, conflicts that hamper productivity, and situations that foster a toxic workplace.

A few weeks after Margaret talked to Elias, she sent him a complaint letter. In the complaint letter, she provided examples and described the pattern of Brad making decisions that proved harmful for the Wallonia office. Margaret intended to make Elias aware of the situation so he could work towards a "code of conduct" remedy or move her to a new EMEA role internally. Her letter was also intended to protect all employees from more such misconduct and safeguard the group's interests. Elias needed to ensure the protection of new hires and existing employees while being prepared to address such incidents as they might occur in the future.

Below is a content summary of the letter, including suggestions for the development of a code of conduct as a header for each section describing Margaret's concerns:

**Practice integrity; prevent harassment and discrimination in the workplace.**

- Leaders should allow an optimal transition period for new hires. For instance, the handover to Margaret from her predecessor as the Wallonia region's sales manager, Miriam, only took three days. Similarly, Steve from internal sales made the handover to his successor in a transition that took less than a week.

- Leaders should ensure new hires have adequate support during and after the onboarding process from all their co-workers throughout the organisation. For instance, Wallonia employees knew their customers' history, yet no one showed empathy to accommodate a new project manager who nearly suffered from burnout when dealing with a very challenging customer. Margaret experienced this same stress factor. Many of her co-workers understood what Miriam was working on before she left, but they never approached Margaret with this background information or offered any information about it when she asked.

- Leaders should safeguard the group's assets. For instance, when Miriam was permitted to take her laptop when she left the organisation, the organisation lost valuable customer history gathered during the duration of her employment.

- Leaders should work towards a more open communication practice and better employee inclusion. For example, for nearly three years all decisions concerning the Wallonia office were made by Brad, in Antwerp. Margaret carried the responsibility for meeting the target sales revenue for the Wallonia office, and she knew her customers better than anyone in Antwerp. She hoped that by addressing this complaint, leaders would begin including her in matters and decisions concerning the Wallonia office.

- Leaders should ensure that employees and departments work towards a common goal. Margaret requested technical representative support from Paul several times to qualify potential business opportunities, but no help whatsoever was approved. Like many times before, Margaret was left to complete the project herself. Paul didn't show much engagement with or commitment to the Wallonia office. For instance, he had over one year to develop a new product for a customer, but his team didn't complete this task, which resulted in the Wallonia office losing the deal, worth over a million euros, to the competition.

- Meanwhile, there were also the considerable problems with Brad. Brad's bias for his EMEA position over the good of the Wallonia region harmed the group's overall operations, as well as being unfair and stressful to employees like Margaret. Even if he had been entirely fair as a manager, the situation itself was not: Sales are the only department that carries an annual target. The project manager and technical representative have no annual goals or KPIs, yet they dictate when sales obtain resources to deliver revenue results! This was the case in the organisation that employed Margaret, and it meant that salespeople always needed to beg and work tirelessly towards a good working relationship with project managers who then approved or disapproved technical representative resources. Unfortunately, if the project manager remains biased and blocks resources, as Margaret experienced within the

Wallonia office, this relationship weakens until it struggles to exist. Leaders should consider whether all departments of the organisation should receive annual KPI targets to achieve for the group.

- For thirty months, Brad made false and misleading statements by altering Margaret's weekly reports before he sent them to the EMEA leadership team and HQ in the US. This misled EMEA leaders, HQ leaders, the PE firm and their investors, prompting them to disregard any challenges Margaret had before they could even be addressed.

- Leaders should make decisions based on their region of responsibility's best interests. Margaret saw a conflict of interest between international and regional business opportunities and projects because both competed for limited resources. The decision criteria and prioritisation were left for Brad to decide. Who guaranteed that Brad's priorities were set with the group's best interests in mind?

**Praise employees who speak up and practice due diligence.**

- Sooner or later, the truth comes out. However, when the truth came out that Paul had been blocking resources Margaret needed in the Wallonia office, Brad still didn't examine the facts, even though Margaret had informed him of the potential risk to Wallonia's revenue growth several months earlier. Paul's behaviour was revealed when one of Margaret's co-workers, a project manager named David, accidentally mentioned it. Margaret encouraged him to speak to Elias, but David was shaken and said something to the effect of, "I certainly won't speak to Elias and jeopardise my relationship with Paul. It's going to be your word against mine!" This showed the truth of David's character and the environment of fear Paul created in his departments.

**Value employees and treat them fairly.**

- Wallonia's sales revenue continued to grow even though the office remained understaffed. They were profitable, and since the job was getting done with fewer people on the payroll, they saved costs. However, Margaret found it disappointing that Brad cancelled eighty hours of her overtime. This overtime helped Wallonia generate revenue and build its sales pipeline, and it arose because, unlike many other regions, the Wallonia office was not provided adequate French and German-speaking department support in the pre-sales or post-sales phases. Margaret had continued working to address that challenge for over thirty months.

- Successful and healthy companies offer fair pay and compensate those who deliver results that matter. Margaret had consistently shown integrity and produced those results. However, after nearly thirty months, she felt Brad and the leadership team didn't acknowledge the value she brought to the table, as witnessed by the miniscule salary increases she had received: 1.25% after the first year on the job and only 1.1% in the second year.

**Help employees to explore options, raise issues, and address concerns.**

- Departments should share the workload and responsibilities throughout the entire sales cycle. However, Margaret had learned that more structured departments with detailed engagement processes could quickly push their workload and responsibilities back to the sales department, who had few resources and no comprehensive sales engagement process.

- Steps should have been taken to reduce or avoid duplicate workload, such as Brad's weekly reporting requirements through Excel and OneNote and the non-sales activities that came with the French language barrier. Margaret needed to do her job in developing business, not be involved in roles and responsibilities for departments such as credit & collections, customer care, contract management, marketing, and procurement.

- The organisation overlooked opportunities to inject speed and accuracy into its processes to shorten the sales cycle, improving speed from quotation to order while remaining in line with the group's "Get things right, every time" attitude. Specifically, Margaret suggested they could:

  ➢ Reduce the time to get higher discount pricing approved by leadership from two weeks to a few days. This delay didn't only prolong the sales cycle, but it negatively impacted cash flow, earnings, and customer experience.

  ➢ "Get it right the first time" – the first impression matters. Sales spent a lot of time on administrative tasks because they needed to get each task in the proposal phase right the first time before submitting a proposal to a customer. A lot of work is necessary for the qualification period and the proposal submission period (presales phase). As a result, when the customer returned the signed proposal, the back office could efficiently process the order internally from there on out. This was just one reason why it was so crucial for salespeople to receive more presales support from technical, engineering, legal counsel, and throughout the organisation than they had up to now.

  ➢ Spend maximum time on selling and closing new business deals. A software tool that automates time-consuming tasks could eliminate the need for the sales team to reinvent the wheel constantly. For instance, they could create quotes easily and efficiently by finally upgrading the CRM to make the quote development process an integral part of the sales process. Additionally, the group could use a pricing model that allowed sales to pick products and prices, add discount levels, and then submit the offer without having to leave the CRM tool. As a result, they would deliver professional quotes to ensure that corporate identity is maintained. The business proposals that sales created varied from region to region and directly influenced customer experience and perception. The organisation needed a cohesive and professional impression to enhance their brand.

**Make value-based decisions.**

- It must be straightforward to get leadership's attention (via email, phone, text, or other ways) so they could take the action required to minimise business risks. Furthermore, it was important for leadership to consider feedback they received from employees with first-hand experience. Paul's decision not to change an overwhelmed project manager, despite Margaret's recommendation to do so, ended up causing delays and rising costs, including missed and lost deals. Until the overwhelmed project manager was replaced eighteen months later, Margaret was occupied by offering project management support to help with this work. Her efforts may have solved Paul's project management challenges, but the organisation's business development challenges had to go unaddressed during this period.

After sending the complaint letter, Margaret was relieved and hoped this would lead to some remedy for the problems, thus protecting other employees and maybe even the future success of the organisation.

A few weeks later, Elias set up a meeting with Margaret at a service station restaurant to discuss her letter and go over next steps. The first question Margaret asked in their meeting was about her status to be transferred. The idea of a transfer had crossed her mind, but she hadn't been able to address this concern with anyone, nor could she ask to be moved to another position, because no HR existed before Elias came. Now she wanted to know: if she left her manager, Brad, would that mean she had to leave the organisation? Elias explained that he needed to get all the facts before considering possible options. To get a better understanding, he wanted to first speak with Brad. Elias suggested setting up a meeting between Brad, Margaret, and himself, which Margaret understood. She appreciated Elias's neutrality and looked forward to an opportunity to improve the circumstances of her position or move internally to a new job. She agreed to have this first meeting to seek a dialogue that would create a better atmosphere and help them to move forward.

While they were at the service station restaurant going through the points in the complaint letter, Margaret also showed Elias all the documents and communication she had gathered as evidence of Brad's misconduct. Elias told her to keep these documents at hand until he decided to begin an internal investigation. These documents are still with Margaret today.

As the meeting came to an end, Margaret recalled how she had heard about a new opening as Head of EMEA Sales. She asked Elias if she could be considered for it. Elias seemed slightly irritated that Margaret knew about this open position. He advised her to apply for a marketing position that would shortly be communicated within EMEA, and she agreed to apply as soon as she got the job advertisement. The meeting ended, and both left the restaurant.

The following day, Elias shared the marketing position via an email to Margaret only. Since the marketing department was also under Innovation, the new marketing role would have to report to Paul as CTO. The same week, Margaret submitted her CV to Paul. A week later, Paul and Margaret had their first (and last) interview in Antwerp. In Margaret's opinion, the interview went well, but unfortunately, Paul rejected her candidacy for the marketing position. Margaret asked if he could name other employees who applied for this position, but he wasn't willing to share any further details with her. She later learned that the job opening she had applied to had already been given to someone else in the organisation long before she was interviewed. Troubled with this situation, Margaret wondered why this was never internally communicated. If either Elias or Paul knew that this position was already for someone else, then why bother giving Margaret an interview, wasting everyone's time and the organisation's money?

# Chapter 8

# A Toxic Workplace Loses All

## Making a Stand

Nearly six months passed, and nothing more happened regarding the complaint letter. Rather than seeing improvements, Margaret had to watch as the situation only continued to worsen. Elias didn't seem to take her seriously. She felt that leaders tended to stick together in these situations, and she thought Elias was not working towards the group's best interest. Instead, he was working with Brad's best interests in mind. She believed everyone, including the leaders who lacked integrity, should be held accountable. Only then would there be a corporate culture change within the organisation.

Margaret was very successful in her Wallonia office, and she was not planning to leave. She was ready to stay and fight for other employees. However, she had felt like the underdog for so long. Enough was enough. Margaret wrote a second letter (below) to report the "Factors Negatively Impacting the Revenues" with the request for an internal investigation into Brad's misconduct and the fact that he obstructed progress. She included a presentation with her second complaint letter that had seven slides with the following topics:
1. Factors reducing revenue
2. SWOT analysis of the Wallonia region
3. The Wallonia region's sales pipeline
4. Proposed sales strategy for her region
5. Lessons learned from the Wallonia region
6. Margaret's KPIs in the last three years

7. Root cause analysis summary of Brad's approaches which obstructed growth and innovative enhancements in the Wallonia region

Margaret was sure something was not right, and the misconduct in the organisation went against her principles, morals, and integrity as an employee, but she was still unable to confirm that judgment without a thorough internal investigation, which she wrote to request. Below is a summary of the second letter, which Margaret sent six months after the first.

*Dear Elias,*

*July 27, 2012, will be my third year with the organisation as a sales manager (French and German community region). I have tried to bring my complaint to your attention (in my previous letter) to no avail. Therefore, I'm writing to submit a formal complaint letter to report factors negatively impacting revenue, with the request for an internal examination or investigation of Brad for his misconduct, constant biased behaviour, and business-blocking activities towards the Wallonia region.*

*I sincerely hope this letter offers a fair chance to put the facts straight by presenting six approaches Brad took to obstruct Wallonia's growth. These have resulted in substantial losses, missed opportunities, lower profitability, and lower productivity, including delaying EMEA's enhancement. I would estimate the cost of these losses over the past thirty months to be a figure in the millions of dollars. Further, after my first complaint letter nearly six months ago, the situation has only worsened, and I herewith seek an internal transfer to a different job. Please let me know possible internal positions for my transfer.*

*Every employee has to exercise due diligence, get their facts and evidence straight, question the status quo, challenge it when necessary, and even criticise those*

*wanting to harm the Wallonia region. I'm not with the organisation to outshine anyone or to destroy someone's status. I'm doing my part by trying to offer the best of what I do well. Even though I've experienced exclusion, defamation of character in the workplace, and labelling by individual leaders, I have been faithful to what I believe integrity requires.*

*Despite all odds against me, I have still achieved high KPIs in the Wallonia region, enabling it to stand out compared to other regions of the organisation. I've generated double-digit millions in revenue in the last three years, and I've established double-digit millions in a robust sales pipeline. In my opinion, I've protected and safeguarded the interests of the organisation for nearly three years now.*

*If I weren't confident enough to request a thorough internal examination or investigation of the ways Brad has obstructed progress for the organisation, I would not have made the effort of writing this letter. I hope the PE firm evaluates the root cause analysis and agrees on an internal investigation, and if the organisation and investors are confident after the investigation that the facts do not establish Brad's guilt, I will gracefully resign from my position in the next three months.*

*I hope to hear from you soon.*
*Sincerely,*
*Margaret*

The following summary provides a better understanding of the challenges and core factors that were reducing earnings, not only at Margaret's region in Wallonia but for Belgium as a whole. It offers a case study of how one toxic workplace negatively affected revenue. The below case study illustrates the due diligence practiced by Margaret.

## Root Cause Analysis

**Business strategy challenges**

Not much effort was made to update the organisation's business strategy after M&A combined more than a dozen affiliated brands. The business strategy needed review to ensure its continued success in the altered external and internal environments. Margaret provided a SWOT analysis with her region's results to Brad at the end of her second year, after she monitored how the strategy and the objectives were being executed in the organisation and the entire group, so she had some insight into this.

<u>Internal power struggle</u>: Margaret observed Brad's power struggles within the group. Instead of rational, value-making decisions, these led to political choices that did not benefit the group as a whole. For example, Margaret and Brad were at an international sales meeting in London where ten other EMEA salespeople were present, and one of the affiliated brands of the group, a former competitor, had presented their software. Even though the ten EMEA salespeople were impressed with the software, Brad insisted that he wasn't going to sell this affiliated brand's software in his regions, which included the Wallonia region. Brad's statement at the sales meeting was in line with the view Margaret had of the three CEOs of other affiliated brands which used to be competitors: she suspected they would react similarly. Margaret thought salespeople, when they qualified a business opportunity, would first examine the possibility that one of the four former competitors might have a solution in their product portfolio the customer wanted. Instead, Brad preferred to start long-lasting product development projects for one specific customer, projects which were not linked to the overall PLM of the business strategy. Such resource-consuming projects meant EMEA salespeople continued to experience a conflict of interest between international and regional projects for the limited remaining resources needed to close their deals. There was still no guarantee that the CEOs of the formerly competing brands would instruct their salespeople to position the group's entire product portfolio, even if this

was the most beneficial approach for the whole of the group. Margaret was confident that after the M&A of the first three competitors, there had not been any organisational change management. Therefore, plenty of competition and power struggles continued between them. A contributing factor was that headquarters in the US still allocated annual revenue targets by affiliated brand instead of by region or product group. Naturally, then, each CEO had to ensure the revenue targets for their brand were achieved. The pressure to meet short-term goals, combined with the internal power struggle among leadership, led to an autocratic management style and poor employee engagement. Rather than being proactive, employees failed to practice due diligence, and several spread defamation in the workplace. In this way, Brad and other leaders allowed a toxic and unproductive work environment to prosper.

<u>Business models</u>: The leaders of the dozen affiliated brands were all occupied with achieving their individual targets and didn't see the urgency to re-evaluate a business model for the entire group. There were no specific business models in place for OEM customers versus large enterprise customers, public customers, and strategic alliances and partnerships. Not only Belgium, but the group overall seemed to be missing a strategic business model.

<u>Code of conduct</u>: Margaret was sure no written code of conduct existed in any of the affiliated brands, let alone one for the group. Meanwhile, one of the most alarming challenges throughout the organisation was the fear of speaking up. Margaret, like many other employees, was afraid to lose her job as Brad and other leaders began to exhibit a more autocratic management style. No one wanted to challenge these leaders, speak out against them, or even practice due diligence. Naturally, employees feared being negatively labelled by CEOs, leaders, managers, co-workers, groups, and departments in their organisation and throughout the group of affiliated

brands. In some nasty cases, leaders made work difficult until the targeted employees finally decided to leave the organisation on their own, until they were admitted to a burnout clinic, or until they were discharged under false pretences.

<u>Colliding brands and culture:</u> To make the group more attractive for sale, the PE firm leadership decided first to create consistency in the corporate identity. A plan was set forth accordingly and continued for many years, including the years Margaret worked within the group, but information about this plan wasn't well-distributed and no one was living the development of the brand consistency. The CEOs of the dozen affiliated brands were supposed to scrap all their product brand names and focus on developing one new brand for the entire group. They would then consolidate all hardware and software product developments to have one product development team for the whole group instead of nearly a dozen. Consequently, the CEOs of the group, including Brad, were losing power, and they were no longer flexible with product development like they had been in the past. These CEOs operated in fear of being demoted, of not achieving their individual brand's revenue targets and KPIs, and worse, of losing their jobs due to possible organisational change management initiatives. The lack of change management pre- and post-M&A, including the internal power struggle between the four formerly competing affiliated brands, had a great toll on synergy and collaboration among employees of all dozen brands. Leadership's resistance to change slowed, opposed, and obstructed all change management efforts which the final investors were hoping the PE firm and the organisation would achieve. However, to ensure success in the positioning of the group's product portfolio, during the final two years of her job, Margaret spent 60% of her sales activity time growing Brad's branded products, while the remaining 40% was to position the entire group's product portfolio. In twenty months, she developed a double-digit-

million-euro sales pipeline, in which 30% of the business opportunities were for products from other affiliated brands, including the three former competitors.

<u>All departments working towards a common goal with KPIs:</u> The salesperson is not in finance, human resources, engineering, product management, project management, or operations. They are salespeople, paid to generate revenue and grow profits by reaching out to customers and prospects – meaning their KPIs should be the organisation's top priority. The product manager, project manager, or technical representative has no annual targets or KPIs, yet they can dictate when sales obtain resources to deliver results. Leaders should consider whether the sales department leads in growing the business and other departments follow, or all departments of the organisation get annual KPI targets to achieve that are complimentary to the salespersons' KPIs. If leaders don't think salespeople should dictate when they require technical resources, then these leaders need to re-evaluate the possibility of creating a team target to achieve rather than leaving only the salesperson with an annual sales revenue target to achieve.

<u>Lack of active investor involvement:</u> Russell Reynold, with Green Peak, developed six recommendations for private equity leaders; in doing this, he observed and countered six flawed assumptions. The third is that "Active investor involvement means I'm failing." On the contrary, Reynold points out that "if we [investors] don't know about a problem, then we can't help, and often we do have resources and ideas that actually can help – and we want to." The group's current reporting policy diluted accountability, and for over three years, Brad had tampered with Margaret's weekly sales reports before sending them to the EMEA leadership and the US headquarters. The PE firm and its investors were misinformed and not actively involved enough.

<u>Lessons learned from past years:</u> After one year on the job, Margaret provided EMEA leaders with a lessons-

learned summary of the past three years' decline in revenue growth year-on-year (YoY). After extracting customer history from the ERP system and speaking with co-workers, she learned that in the previous three years, the overall group's growth had fluctuated. Still, Wallonia revenue continued to decline year-on-year until Margaret came. Margaret was confident that the decline in Wallonia's revenue under Miriam began when Brad started allocating all resource budgets meant for Wallonia to his EMEA sales region. Brad continued with this approach after Margaret replaced Miriam.

<u>Mergers & acquisitions aftermath:</u> The aftermath of M&A always impacts employees, and this group had gone through several M&As to grow to a dozen different brands and their product portfolios. Overall, the group had nearly one thousand employees who had not experienced onboarding or change management for many years. The last of four competitors to be acquired was the organisation where Margaret worked. Combined, the four former competitors had an extensive product portfolio that could cover up to 80% of customer demand worldwide. However, they also had many unfinished product developments that sales could not position in their markets because, when these several M&As took place without an onboarding process, it negatively impacted product development activities and hampered the progress of all affiliated brands' innovation.

<u>Narcissistic leadership style and ostracism:</u> Margaret remembered the conversation in which Brad said that he never wanted to be the CEO of the Belgium organisation but was forced to take the role. Everyone should have the liberty to reject an offer if it doesn't come with adequate success factors or benefits. Margaret, for instance, resigned from her role as Belgium sales director to better serve the organisation. After Margaret resigned from that role and Brad noticed the success her region was achieving when she positioned the group's entire product portfolio, he started making additional efforts to

complicate the situation. He put up further barriers to Margaret's success, which was also the success of the PE firm and its investors. Brad's desire was to show investors his best performance achievements as EMEA sales director, and he did this by taking credit for work Margaret completed while simultaneously showing investors that her performance was unproductive. Brad did this to cover up his failures as his emphasis on his international sales team lead to neglect for the position that was forced upon him as a CEO responsible for 110 employees in Belgium.

<u>Leaders blocked resources Margaret needed for presales activities:</u> During a phone call with Brad more than two years into the job, Margaret told him that Paul was blocking the resources she needed for her presales activities and stated that the constant dispute and toxicity in the Wallonia office had made it unproductive, so she would work remotely until the issue was solved. She informed him about the potential risk that all this chaos would impact sales' win ratio and requested that he look into this employee disengagement concern. Instead of getting better, things got worse. A few weeks after this call with Brad, the truth came out in the Wallonia office when David accidentally told Margaret and three other employees that Paul mentioned he would block resources Margaret needed to succeed. Margaret advised David to speak to Elias about what Paul told him, but David refused for fear of risking his own relationship with Paul. Though Margaret understood the concern that motivated him, she couldn't agree with his inaction, which seemed to show a lack of basic integrity and principles.

<u>Brad's lack of risk evaluation and management:</u> Brad involved individuals and teams in his efforts to further complicate life for Margaret. For example, a group of employees visited two Wallonia customers and set up a customer event without Margaret's knowledge. Even after a meeting with Elias, Brad denied having involved this team. Yet a co-worker confirmed in an email that Brad

knew about his team's visits to customers in Wallonia. Neither Brad nor these employees examined the possible negative consequences this might have had to the limited customer base in Wallonia. For instance, a recently won deal had nearly caused a disaster to the customer because Brad's team wanted to position a non-certified product. Luckily Margaret intervened and sold the customer a product from an affiliated brand that was certified and future-proof. This future-proof solution was the first of its type sold in Belgium, and today this customer remains a great reference.

*Margaret's summary of Brad's misconduct stated that:*

The evidence for Brad's actions and intent to delay Wallonia's progress required a more in-depth investigation, whether conducted by in-house human resources or outside counsel. Additionally, the evidence also suggested that Rachael and Paul were complicit with Brad's misconduct. These leaders joined forces with Brad to construct complex processes and practices among departments that benefitted a few and annoyed the rest. Furthermore, they were regularly involved in efforts to slow the advancement of progress in Wallonia. These efforts involved different strategies put in place over many months or years with the goal to perhaps delay the sale of the group from the PE firm's portfolio. Many of the leaders looked forward to their retirement in the next few years; for them, it would make sense to slow down progress so their remaining careers would be predictable. Meanwhile, all leaders of these colliding cultures and brands, now belonging to a single group, were working hard to keep the lights on for their brand, rather than the dozen affiliated brands working towards building a unified strategy for the entire group.

Brad added tension to an already toxic environment: For example, he forwarded sensitive emails meant only for his eyes to other employees, causing more stress and bias in the workplace.

Brad allocated resource budgets meant for Wallonia to other regions: Margaret's region's business progress was hindered as her boss continued to tamper with her ability to perform her job. She felt her region was predestined to fail, lacking sufficient workforce resources for smooth and hassle-free execution of her tasks for revenue growth. The resources for the Wallonia office hardly ever helped close a deal, nor did they provide technical engineering support on business opportunities in the presales phase. The Antwerp office employees were meant to help all sales regions under Brad, but of the different sales regions, just 5% of Antwerp employee's workload was for Wallonia. Yet on average, Wallonia accounted for 35% of the organisation's total annual sales revenue for Belgium. This revenue was earned despite the French-language barrier, while the lack of support had much to do with the bias Brad had against Margaret and her region's office. Although Wallonia had resource budgets, Brad reallocated them to the EMEA area where his bonus incentive was valued, and he did this three years in a row.

Margaret had no decision-making authority over her region: Brad's efforts seemed to ensure not only that she lacked this authority, but that Wallonia became an unprofitable high-cost centre and a very toxic place for a salesperson in the long term. He made all decisions for Wallonia without Margaret's accord. Many of these decisions failed to add value. For instance, he did not replace the project manager for a top customer, which delayed millions in revenue. Another example was the lack of legal counsel provided when she needed to close an SLA deal for a customer, a lack that led to the organisation missing out on two years of recurring revenue from services. Margaret carried all the pressure to meet Wallonia's revenue target and all the responsibilities, plus all the stress, and she knew her customers better than anyone in the organisation, but she still had no input on what decisions were best for the Wallonia office.

Brad made biased statements about Margaret: Brad made statements about Margaret that led to her being shunned by co-workers, as well as altering her weekly sales reports before sending them to the EMEA leadership and HQ in the US. As a result, many executives were misinformed about her and could not relate to the specific challenges Margaret faced in her sales region. The toxicity Margaret dealt with each day was beyond acceptable, especially in the nine months when she was forced to work remotely to avoid it from co-workers and leaders. No amount of money could quantify the cost to her self-worth.

**Process challenges**

<u>Proper handovers for new hires:</u> Rapid handovers such as the one between Miriam and Margaret were not a phenomenon limited to the sales department in Wallonia, because the same thing happened to Steve from internal sales in Antwerp. Mismanaging employee handovers in this way prolonged the time it took for the new employees to clearly understand the business and participate in it. New salespeople didn't know what business opportunities or projects their predecessors recently won for them to work on, or what challenges the region faced. As a newcomer, Margaret had little to no customer history and was confronted by unhappy customers. She had no sales pipeline overview, and projects were delayed by a lack of appropriate project management resources, along with the lack of legal support she experienced in working to close SLA deals.

<u>Decision criteria for allocating scarce resources:</u> EMEA salespeople continued to see a conflict of interest between international and regional projects because both sales teams were in constant competition for limited resources needed to close their deals. Many EMEA salespeople shared a frustration at this situation. Their leadership needed a course of action to mitigate the long-term damages for customers, who were not well-served through the conflict and lack of resources, because EMEA

could not afford to lose them at this rate and at the same time expect the group to become a billion-euro organisation.

<u>Sales engagement process (presales support):</u> The presales qualification phase was resource-intensive, and winning deals has always been a team effort. Margaret suffered stress from a lack of support during the presales phase and from too many non-sales activities, both of which created a workload that was unproductive. In the presales phase, salespeople need assistance from several parts of the organisation to win new business. Then, when a salesperson closes a complicated deal with multiple components, integration, and commissioning, they need support from the engineering department to handle fulfilment. In most organisations, the commercial salesperson manages the value proposition and negotiations to close the deal, while the technical department puts the value proposition into practice. The technical representative assess the customer's technological needs and evaluates a technical solution the customer wants.

<u>Brad created an internal sales process that only benefited his international sales team:</u> In the presales phase, the rest of his EMEA sales team was supposed by a technical representative who developed the technical drawing and completed the technical configuration of the proposal. This wasn't the case for Margaret's region, even though Wallonia was part of Brad's EMEA sales region. Brad gave the French-language barrier as a reason why a different sales approach was necessary for Wallonia. This only made it more complicated for Margaret. For instance, she had to submit the proposal to the end customer herself when a business opportunity was qualified for another affiliated brand of the group. This process didn't apply to other sales regions. In those regions, when a business opportunity was qualified for an affiliated branded product, the affiliated brand's salesperson would directly submit the proposal to the end customer. It was

frustrating to imagine how many more man-hours and money EMEA was willing to lose every day, as a group, in this sales engagement process, and even more frustrating for Margaret to ask herself, why don't leaders make more of an effort to shape a holistic sales engagement process by first speaking with salespeople from each EMEA region? Then, as Brad took notice of Margaret's success in winning more deals, and her increased synergies with other affiliated brands of the group, he began to involve the individuals within those affiliated brands in constructing more policies and processes that prolonged and complicated the sales process for Wallonia.

The sales engagement process for the entire group: Each of the CEOs of the affiliated brands created their own regional sales engagement process, and as mentioned, this benefited only Brad's international sales team. For example, a technical representative helped Brad's international sales team develop technical drawings and complete the proposal configuration sent to clients. In this way, they helped the salespeople in the presales phase – which wasn't the case for Margaret's region in Wallonia. Meanwhile, Margaret identified patterns behind why customers were unhappy and why revenue continued to decline. As she put the puzzle pieces together, she learned that four years before she began working with the organisation, the presales support for the Wallonia office suddenly changed. The sales engagement process with other departments had also shifted from its original state. For instance, there were no longer internal salespeople who helped the external salesperson in back-office activities and the proposal development phase. Also, they no longer had access to the technical representative who used to help salespeople in the presales phase to qualify the technical feasibility of an end-to-end solution.

Additionally, Brad's conduct alongside Paul to adopt an EMEA sales engagement process showed a lack of due diligence. At an international sales meeting in Barcelona,

Paul (on behalf of Brad) presented an EMEA sales engagement process. This process wasn't designed to shorten the sales cycle. It was complicated, it didn't consider selling other affiliated brands' products because a project manager had developed it for project management rather than sales, and to Margaret's understanding, this sales engagement process was never tested for success in any EMEA sales region. Why didn't Brad explore other options that had been tested and proven successful in other regions – for instance, the Wallonia sales engagement process?

**Product innovation and training challenges**

<u>Employee product knowledge and continued training:</u> As a result of the leadership's internal power struggle, the salespeople, including technical representatives, project managers, and product managers, in each affiliated brand lacked knowledge about products from the other affiliated brands. This delayed market awareness in the development of the group's new cohesive brand. Generally, very few employees had a holistic understanding of the group's entire product portfolio because they lacked continued department-specific training programs. During a financial year when Margaret focused on closing as many deals for all affiliated brands of the group as she could, she was left without any technical representative support who knew the group's product portfolio. Margaret made a point to plan frequent hardware and software training for herself and other staff, but once Brad found out, he requested that the training be cancelled without giving a reason for this request. The internal power struggle among leadership was accompanied by the pressure to meet short-term goals for their individual brands, and all of this without Margaret being given adequate resources to achieve these goals.

<u>Product transition strategy and product lifecycle management:</u> Margaret provided Paul with a product transition strategy and product lifecycle management

approach to use for the organisation because he lacked experience in PLM. She later learned that this strategy and approach were accordingly implemented for the group, giving it tools which never existed before.

**Tool challenges**

<u>Tools for the job:</u> Adequate tools for the job were missing. For instance, no ERP tool for the visual communication sector existed. The web-based ERP tool the organisation purchased was suitable for the cosmetics industry, but not for the visual communication business sector. This made it impossible to create a complete solution or a complex configuration proposal for customers. Instead, all proposals were sent in pdf-converted Word, Excel, or PowerPoint documents.

The ERP tool was also missing product and component pricing because the organisation had no strategic pricing model. Therefore, in many instances, Margaret had to send a request to procurement to get the required product pricing activated in the ERP tool. Three years before Margaret came to work in Wallonia, the EMEA leadership had been in the process of implementing a new ERP tool for the group, with a CRM tool implementation to follow soon after. Despite these plans, the implementation still had not been completed six years later, by which point Margaret included it in her complaint letter.

In addition to the lacking ERP tool, the organisation did not have any CRM tool to archive customer data (contact details, installed base, names of decision-makers, decision-making process, etc.) or to track customer interactions and activities (e.g. customer meeting reports, project status, weekly sales reporting, SOW, or notes on the sales pipeline and leads for potential business opportunities). Even though Brad, Rachael, and Paul knew the US headquarters had already implemented Pega CRM, they were evaluating the possibility of implementing a different CRM tool. Margaret proposed to them that it would reduce costs and increase productivity to have the same CRM tool as the HQ because sales records would be instantly visible. In hindsight, Margaret assumed this direct reporting was something Brad feared because he'd lose control over what information he would and would not share. Rachael, however, requested her help on this CRM initiative. Margaret prepared a CRM questionnaire for employees, prepared CRM user groups in the organisation, and created a best practice method for the weekly sales reporting process as part of the CRM initiative. However, Rachael communicated to employees that after its six-year attempt, EMEA had failed to implement the ERP for the group. This automatically impacted the Pega CRM implementation, further delaying it another three to five years. Brad and other leaders' actions continue to mislead investors and potentially to lose millions over the next three to five years. The leaders had then communicated that the group would re-evaluate a new ERP initiative, but Margaret questioned what would be different this time to ensure success on a second attempt.

**People challenges**

Hiring the right skill sets: Margaret was stunned by the apparent lack of motivation to hire people with the right skill set to support the organisations and her sales region. Favouritism, including nepotism, was another issue she identified. Several new hires had critical roles within the organisation without having the right qualifications or competencies to perform their tasks successfully. For example, a new project manager was hired and assigned to a top customer who had awarded the Wallonia office a contract to install five hundred visual communication solutions out of a potential five thousand solutions – a significant business opportunity. This was the overwhelmed project manager Margaret had supported when Brad and Paul disregarded her suggestion to transfer him to a different project. Brad and Paul were aware that the organisation was not progressing with the product development and the project implementations for this customer. However, they still did not see the need to hire or allocate adequate resources. Margaret knew she had less than two years left to close eight of the nine different deals of the remaining 4,500 installations. It became clear that even though she had all the stress that came with meeting the sales quotas, she had no decision authority whatsoever. Her opinion was weighted very low as a sales manager responsible for a sales region. Even with all odds against her, Margaret managed to close eight out of nine deals, worth a double-digit-million-euro figure, within the customer's expected deadlines. The ninth deal, Margaret lost against a competitor because her organisation innovation team was unable to develop a compatible product within one year.

<u>Language barrier</u>: The lack of French-speaking support for departments in Wallonia and Antwerp continued to cause hidden costs. Less than 1% of the entire workforce spoke French or German. Everyone else spoke either Dutch or English. Margaret had a heavy burden of translation work for every communication with French-speaking customers. She quickly realised that she didn't have the luxury of extra time like salespeople in regions who didn't face the language challenge. Margaret couldn't work efficiently with either customers or the organisation's internal operations as she always had to translate everything.

## The Value of Corporate Culture

The previous chapters have described how Margaret mapped out specific sales performance challenges, closely examining how sales performance had evolved in the workplace environment pre- and post-M&A. Margaret became curious about the value of corporate culture in her organisation and group. She knew she needed business intelligence to complete the root cause analysis that would quantify the earnings realised with a happy workplace –

or as had happened in hers, the missed earnings with a toxic one.

The following factors helped Margaret gather the data that revealed a potential earnings loss of 50+% over thirty months in her toxic workplace:

- Her approach in the first three months to learn the ERP tool, from which she extracted customer revenue history from the past three years, provided Margaret with useful information and helped her understand what strategic action to take to grow revenue further and to prevent further loss of market share.
- Her approach in the first twelve months of speaking to as many employees as possible, even employees of the other affiliated brands, helped her not only to build initial rapport and learn the ins and outs of the group, but also to get a bigger picture of the group's and organisation's business strategy, challenges they faced, and what she could actually control as a salesperson.
- After nearly thirty months on the job, Margaret had identified a sales revenue benchmark that her region could achieve. With this benchmark, she quantified the revenue performance impact by identifying patterns of employee disengagement, including evaluating the characters and mindset of these disengaged employees compared to the employees who remained engaged with the group's overall vision and mission statement. Positive and negative revenue performance results correlated, respectively, to engaged and disengaged employees' behavioural patterns. She then calculated the employee salary costs for her region and the delayed project implementation revenues, including the lost deals and the potential sales missed due to her being occupied in supporting project management over eighteen months. She deducted these impacts from the sales revenue benchmark her region could achieve. Her calculations resulted in

figure over 50% below that benchmark, which is an extraordinary value, even considering that it comes from an extreme case of a toxic workplace – especially since that percentage is only from the sales department. The 50+% decline in potential earnings didn't include the impact the toxic workplace had on other departments at the same time.

- The overall conclusion: A happy workplace is a vital success factor for overall sales performance, which is, in turn, a critical differentiating factor to the bottom-line success or failure of an organisation. A happy workplace shortens product time to market, creates an efficient sales cycle, and produces cost-effective benefits for other parts of the organisation as well. A toxic workplace elongates these factors, creating costly, lengthy product time to market and inefficient sales activities.

The measurement of something as complex and unclassifiable as an organisation's corporate culture has been a matter of much debate. Some argue that corporate culture must be intuitively sensed rather than measured, while others say the best way to uncover an organisation's corporate culture is learning from ethnographic studies that had been conducted and analysing the stories and accounts of situations which make up the folklore of every organisation. The measured value of 50+% described here takes a different approach in quantitatively measuring corporate culture, one created by Margaret, while also drawing from an ethnographic account: Margaret's experience forms a case study of its own.

### Conclusion of the Root Cause Analysis

As a salesperson, Margaret didn't worry about things she couldn't change; instead, she focused on the one thing she could change, and that was the customer experience. She could impact this by doing her job to the best of her abilities and by reporting to and advising her organisation's leaders on potential risks, weakness, and opportunities.

The effort Margaret expended in conducting the root cause analysis was done to provide insights for further studies to follow. She believed that with a root cause analysis performed to produce a list of lessons learned and acquired knowledge, the organisation could conduct further analysis and develop fishbone diagrams, which show the causes of a specific event, more efficiently.

Within the analysis she conducted, several aspects of the organisation's operational excellence and the engagement of departments in the business development cycle were examined over thirty months. The analysis was an amalgamation of different best-practice methods and approaches, and a fishbone diagram was provided to display all possible root cause challenges accordingly.

Margaret identified the leading root causes as "Lack of expertise/knowledge around best-practice business development methods" and "Lack of knowledge in innovation/product lifecycle management." The combination of these and other challenges created a chain reaction of unfortunate events and somewhat "unforeseen circumstances." For instance, first, you had Brad's misconduct towards Margaret and the Wallonia region. Second, you had the internal power struggle among the affiliated brand's leadership. Third, you had the individual annual revenue targets each affiliated brand had to achieve; this did nothing to promote cooperation among the dozen affiliated brands, which included four former competitors. Fourth, you had colliding cultures and brands who lacked strategic business guidance from leaders. Fifth and most important, you had employees who were never considered in the M&A equation and who never experienced change management within the group.

While the root cause analysis did not prove Brad's lack of integrity in his decision-making process towards the Wallonia region, it also did not declare his innocence. Based on the evidence gathered about Brad's actions, including the factors reducing revenues, Margaret was unable to be confident in her judgment without a thorough investigation by Elias.

# Chapter 9

# A Political Climate Obstructs Innovative Enhancements

Brad's misuse and abuse of power reminded Margaret of a childhood memory she had of confronting a bully in school, where she discovered the power of character and empathy.

She was fourteen years old and attending an international school in Brussels. With gorgeous sports fields, plus a state-of-the-art facility with a beautiful swimming pool, this was an ideal location for a Hollywood school movie. Inside her class, however, things were not as nice. One student, Jane, was well known to be a bully and called the less popular kids all kinds of names.

"I remember Jane as a chubby girl, and how she walked like a ruffian seeking her next victim to bully," Margaret recalled. "Jane reminded me of Rasputia Latimore from the 2007 American comedy movie *Norbit*. Once, at a school lunch, Jane grabbed another girl, Monica, by the shirt and threw her against a nearby wall. Monica fell to the ground, and Jane kicked her while she was down. 'Stay down,' she said, though in a more colourful language."

Margaret was sitting nearby listening to her Walkman as things played out. At some point she had seen enough of Jane's bullying, and she intervened. Margaret pushed Jane back as she prepared to kick Monica again. Jane knew Margaret was a karate and boxing student who had been in many ring fights, and Jane never dared to bully her. Still, she was shocked that anyone would go against her and stand up for Monica. From then on, Jane did not bully Monica again, and Margaret can't recall Jane or herself getting in trouble, nor for that matter that they ever spoke about what had happened that day. From then on, Jane was cautious with her bullying habits. Whenever she and Margaret saw each other, they both politely nodded, as if to say there existed mutual respect.

All the same, Monica had enough. She called her parents and pleaded with them to take her home for that afternoon. Perhaps she did not need Margaret to intervene after all. Margaret has no idea where Jane or Monica are today, but she likes to think that they are both living equally great lives. It would be untruthful if Margaret refused to admit that she took great pride in using her words, as well as her fists, to stand up for herself and others as a young woman.

Bullying does not affect every child, but it remains an important topic. There is no right formula for when adult intervention is needed or when one should back off. I do think the primary way to address bullying is, whenever possible, to help kids gain individual skills and grow their capacity to figure things out for themselves. However, one of the complexities of bully-victim dynamics in today's world is that they often take place in new areas, such as on the internet or at the workplace. Hopefully, over time, there will emerge people who can be guiding counsellors in these situations because sometimes preadolescents and teenagers – and adults, too – really get in over their heads.

Like school bullying, ostracism, bias, and defamation of character in the workplace cannot always be avoided, but they can be spotted to minimise the risk of happening twice – we must learn to see it and stop it. Every case of bullying between teenagers or working professionals is unique. Yet each one takes a toll on the mental health of the victim, and can even play a role in the suicide rates that affect all age groups in our society today. Therefore, it's essential to provide students and employees with a safe and secure environment where they feel protected. Like teachers and those responsible for our youth, leaders in the workplace need to be observant and model positive, appropriate behaviour.

## The End Game

A few weeks after the second complaint letter was sent, Elias, Brad, and Margaret had their first meeting in Brad's office. Elias opened the meeting by asking Margaret and Brad about their expectations for it. Brad replied that he wanted to hear what Margaret had to say. Margaret had three issues she wanted to address:

    i.    Job openings for which she would be considered.

    ii.    What was required to ensure continued revenue and profitability growth for the Wallonia sales region?

    iii.    What had caused the lack of prioritisation in allocating adequate resources for the Wallonia office?

The meeting went for nearly an hour and a half. When the dialogue on these topics grew intense between Brad and Margaret, Elias jumped in and suggested that they set an action plan in which both of them would complete certain tasks within a given timeframe. They agreed on two activities, and the progress towards achieving them would be evaluated at the second meeting six weeks later. The two activities were:

    (i) Margaret would provide Brad with an updated Excel list containing information about the Wallonia sales pipeline and all customers' contact details. Roughly three days later, Margaret sent this list to Brad.

    (ii) Brad would share the weekly sales report that he usually sent to the EMEA leaders and the headquarters in the US with Margaret's sales reports. However, over the next six weeks, Margaret only received this report once, instead of six times.

After those six weeks, Elias set up the second meeting with Brad and Margaret. That same month, Margaret had closed two significant deals worth millions of euros. She went to the meeting and was baffled to hear she would be discharged. She grew even more bewildered after she heard the reason both Brad and Elias gave verbally for her discharge. After three years of dedication, they said they found her lack of collaboration in the last several months with other staff, departments, and Brad to be very disappointing. During the meeting, Brad admitted the budget allocations that prevented Margaret from acquiring the appropriate resources had been his decision. He also acknowledged the organisational and operational challenges that had contributed to the unpleasant situation in the Wallonia office, and seemed to promise to improve this in the future. Although Margaret was frustrated and disappointed that Elias had not taken her complaint seriously, she gracefully accepted her discharge.

Elias then instructed her to sign two documents that he had prepared. The documents attested that Margaret agreed on the reason for her discharge and that she would be discharged from her position immediately. The documents also stated that during the two-month notice period, Margaret would only have insurance for one month. She refused to sign the two documents without first getting advice from her legal counsel. The meeting soon came to an end, but before leaving the office, Margaret had to leave her laptop and phone with Elias.

A day later, Margaret wrote a letter to Elias in which she requested that the reason for her discharge be sent in writing. Elias sent the letter with the reasons for her discharge three weeks later. The letter asserted a new ground for her discharge, which was a lack of mutual trust so that the contract of employment could no longer be maintained. Margaret wondered why Elias and Brad changed their reason from the verbal one of "lack of collaboration" to the written one of "lack of trust". Why wasn't the reason something else, such as insubordination because Margaret occasionally disagreed with Brad's policies and practices? Margaret knew that changing the reason for her discharge wouldn't change the situation, but the claim about trust was not only untrue, it was an abusive statement and vilification of her person, and she was not willing to accept its damage to her brand as a salesperson in Belgium and Europe.

## The Costs of Due Diligence

The second letter Margaret wrote to Elias about the factors negatively impacting revenue and Brad's approach to obstruct growth in Wallonia may have jeopardised her career at the organisation, but her conscience was clean because she did her job by addressing these issues. Though she was discharged, the employees who remained within the organisation would still be treated differently. The way she spoke up tells a lot about her character. Margaret put herself on the line to protect other employees (and investors) from certain leaders' improper and unacceptable behaviour. The lesson learned from Margaret's story is a message to salespeople and leaders alike to re-evaluate the way we treat each other in working towards inclusion. Narcissistic leaders, and those who build workplaces that foster ostracism, should be concerned about the probability that employees who have had enough of their leaders' misconduct will finally speak up with concrete details about these issues and challenges. In the end, it is usually the employees who experience the brunt of the consequences, including mass layoffs when organisations struggle. This makes it even more likely that salespeople will follow Margaret's example as they conduct these analyses within their own organisations, possibly growing into a movement. Moreover, these challenges are of great interest to every member of the public – not only employees but also investors and labour unions.

Margaret strongly believed that she was wrongfully discharged, and she thought it might have been in retaliation for practicing due diligence and speaking up. Many circumstances around her discharge were also suspect. Compared to his responses to other employees such as Brad, Paul, and many other co-workers who blocked business growth for Margaret's sales region, Elias acted strangely towards her. Was Margaret treated differently and discharged because she was an unusual employee? As for the reason of Margaret's discharge, why had it taken three years to realise her lack of collaboration, or as they now said, trust?

Ordinarily, when an employee contract gets terminated due to misconduct, they usually receive a written warning beforehand. During her three years of employment, Margaret never received a warning notice. An employee must be given the opportunity to explain their behaviour and employers should make efforts to understand their rationale for it. She believed Brad wanted to make her the scapegoat when things went wrong with the revenue growth in Belgium. Before Margaret worked for the organisation, Brad's international business growth was dogged by misfortune. He was forced to take on a CEO position that no one else wanted; he implied that he believed there was no way to revive this brand. Therefore, rather than having a business development strategy to restore and rebuild it, he simply waited for it to perish, and even encouraged that by working on long-lasting projects that burned through money but were never purchased by customers. It seemed that Rachael had hired Margaret for Brad to later discharge her on false grounds, using her supposed failures to cover up his own as he continued to emphasise his international sales team while neglecting the position that was forced upon him as a CEO for Belgium.

There was no better defence than good facts supported by good evidence. For Margaret, enough was enough. For far too long, she had been falsely represented, and she needed to clear her name and her brand.

Everyone is easily replaceable. Brad, Elias, or any leader for that matter, had every right to write off Margaret as an employee. However, because leaders usually stick together, especially in workplaces that have become toxic, workers continue to get discharged every day under false pretences. Margaret believed that if Elias was hired without bias two years before, and she had been able to speak to him earlier, she might have had a fairer outcome. However, Elias was at the right place, but perhaps at the wrong time, with a false assessment of the situation.

What bothered Margaret the most about Elias was that he had less than eight months of insight on the organisation, compared to her thirty-plus months. In her opinion, when she approached Elias with the complaint addressing her concerns, Margaret spoke out in the organisation's best interests. Instead of taking her complaint seriously, Elias helped Brad construct more grounds for Margaret's discharge.


## Engagement Means Employees – and Investors – Flourish

Despite its challenges, Margaret had enjoyed working for the organisation, and, she didn't have another job lined up, nor was she happy to leave the organisation because, in her opinion, while she was doing her job she was also fighting for all employees, not just herself. The misconduct she experienced should not have been tolerated, especially from a leader, but Margaret hoped the PE firm could step in provide much-needed organisational change management.

Over three years as a regional sales manager for Wallonia, Margaret had continued to do her job to the best to her abilities, and this without adequate success factors being allocated to her region. Margaret knew she was loyal to the organisation, not necessarily to a group or to her boss, Brad. Despite her unpleasant experience, Margaret continued to practice due diligence. She had identified opportunities for improvement that resulted in a shorter sales cycle, enhanced efficiency, and increased productivity in collaboration with the group's other affiliated brands. She found ways to increase the effectiveness and positive impact from existing processes and practices. Although Brad's misconduct towards her region made the circumstances difficult, Margaret still overachieved her KPIs and generated profitable revenue for her region.

Margaret was successful in the following:

- On average, every year she had fifty customer visits, including visits conducted to gather business intelligence.
- On average, every year she submitted forty proposals that included tenders. The proposal win/loss ratio was: 44% wins, 32% losses, and 24% on hold or open.
- The win ratio on affiliated branded products sold in her region was 20%.
- On average, every year she attended four exhibitions and invited one customer to the group's factory in Italy.
- On average, every year she attended sixty internal meetings.
- She leveraged forecasts and effectively reported each week on her sales activities.
- She delivered double-digit millions in revenues over three years – growing monthly earnings by double-digit percentages year-on-year, over three years.
- To overachieve her targets, she positioned the group's entire product portfolio of affiliated brands. Simultaneously, she practiced due diligence and identified the potential for improvements by shortening the sales cycle; she reduced costs by 15% in the presales phase when submitting product proposals for the group's affiliated brands to customers.
- Margaret created unique selling propositions twice, for a product and a services package. She created the services package from scratch, and she closed the first service contract deal. All affiliated brand leaders agreed to roll out this services package on a global scale as part of the group's product portfolio for potentially multi-million-euro recurring services revenue streams.
- She established and developed a healthy sales pipeline in the double-digit millions within twenty months.
- She grew SOW earnings on five top customer accounts.

- She closed two future-proof deals; one was the services package she developed from scratch, and the other was an innovative retrofit project that was the first of its kind in Belgium.
- She closed eight out of nine projects with a top customer in twenty months, meeting the customer's stringent deadlines and achieving revenues in double-digit millions.
- The collaboration and synergies between Margaret and the employees of other affiliated brands permitted her to grow revenue for these brands year over year by closing new acquisition deals every four months. She was one of the few salespeople who closed new deals every four months over a three-year period.
- Margaret established and developed a healthy sales pipeline in double-digit millions over a twenty-month period where 30% of the business opportunities were from other affiliated brands of the group.

Despite the remarkable results Margaret achieved even when the odds were stacked against her, when she presented hard evidence on the toxic workplace and the toll it had on her sales region's earnings, she was discharged. Margaret's experience indicates that even though some organisations understand the impact corporate culture has on their success or failure, we still see too many leaders struggle to deliver the right culture fit. Meanwhile, her findings quantified a vast potential value for what corporate culture amounts to.

We can use 50+% as a benchmark for the potential earnings growth realised with a happy workplace, or as the potential decline in revenue due to a toxic work environment.

# Part III
# Strategic Thinking

# Chapter 10

# Sources of Employee Engagement in Happy Workplaces

### The Five Milestones of a Business Development Cycle Explained

We use sales tactics in every interaction in life: whenever we try to capture someone's attention or persuade them to undertake a certain course of action. With sufficient training and practice, everyone can become a business developer. When talking about conceptual sales, however, we primarily refer to an approach to selling products, ideas, solutions, services, and more. Several types of conceptual sales have been crafted for specific business models and market industries, including the business-to-business (B2B) and business-to-consumer (B2C) sectors. At its core, conceptual sales consists of connecting the concept of an end-to-end solution according to the prospective customer's needs. It is a consultative selling approach, in which the customer and salesperson work together to identify needs and solutions. The success of a consultative selling approach depends on the salesperson's attitude and commitment to learning, but also on the organisation's policies and practices.

Every business operates according to its own set of rules, and there is no one-size-fits-all approach when it comes to business development. There are numerous methods in the marketplace that derive real value. Many business developers leaders prefer a specific strategy because it comes naturally to them and fits their particular style. However, first and foremost, the chosen method should reflect the buyer's journey. To avoid missing business opportunities, take the time to learn what motivates your buyers to buy. The next step to tailoring the sales experience for each prospect is to determine the prospect's personality style. Research and collect clues left by the client in your interactions with them, digital and in-person, to find insights into their behaviour, preferences, and decision-making processes.

The below illustration can be used a reference to understand the five milestones in the sales cycle:

| Presales steps | | Task and activities in the sales process |
| --- | --- | --- |
| Presales (Milestone # 1) | Prospect Qualification | - Build rapport with existing customers and establish relationships with new ones |
| | | - Attend product training, internal meetings and calls<br>- Provide direct customer feedback to product development team<br>- Gather insights on market trends and conduct competitor analysis<br>- Complete an assessment of the organisation |
| | | - Research and plan the customer interaction |
| | | - Qualify business opportunities to establish and develop a healthy sales pipeline |
| | | - Create quality reports on customer visits and interactions<br>- Conduct due diligence and risk management to address challenges |
| | | - Plan customer visits and provide actionable, customer-relevant information<br>- Send newsletters with updates on new product launches, product transitions, and roadmaps to customers with signed NDAs<br>- Develop value proposition presentations<br>- Invite customers to workshops and trade shows |

| | | |
|---|---|---|
| | | - Coordinate with a presales technical representative who can assist in answering technical questions and queries, preparing onsite workshops or complex product demonstrations, and training customers on product installations |
| | Prospect disqualification | - At a tender qualification kick-off meeting, allocate bid management resources, including legal evaluation. Disqualify prospects who are not the right fit for the organisation's overall business strategy |
| Presales (Milestone # 2) | Proposal submission | - If required, coordinate design of product concept and solution<br>- Prepare pricing model (price calculations and approvals)<br>- Prepare a win proposal, including cover letter, value proposition, data sheets, and solution design, and get legal counsel for contract management, including a service level agreement (SLA)<br>- Get adequate technical representative support in developing a drawing and configuration of the proposal |
| | | - Plan and coordinate a meeting at the customer's site to present the proposal<br>- Electronically submit the proposal after the onsite presentation |
| Presales (Milestone # 3) | Negotiations | - Was the customer satisfied with the solution proposed, and did the proposal capture their needs? What changes are required in the proposed solution, its services, or the project concept design to move forward? |
| | Commitment to purchase | - What objections (e.g. different solution offering, more services, delivery date, lower price, etc.) need to be addressed before |

| | | |
|---|---|---|
| | | moving forward with a go or no-go response?<br>- Remember to apply a contingency and mitigation plan to control the impact of risks that look likely to occur |
| | Deal is lost or on hold | - Continue to build rapport when the deal is on hold, or even if the deal is lost to a competitor – plus, get feedback on why the competitor won |

| Post-sales steps | | Task and activities in the sales process |
|---|---|---|
| Post-sales (Milestone # 4) | Deal is won | - Send the purchase order to the order processing department and provide customer with confirmation and estimated delivery date(s) |
| | | - Plan kick-off meeting to hand over the deal to the project manager (and project management team)<br>- Project manager takes the lead and begins coordination and rollout implementations, including the use of a project cost management method to measure costs and productivity |
| Post-sales (Milestone # 5) | Develop & retain customer (and begin presales steps again) | - Plan case study (referrals and references) |
| | | - Monitor delivery status and delays, product quality issues, and invoice settlements |
| | | - Monitor escalations to handle complaints rapidly<br>- Provide alternative solutions and follow-up on resolutions |
| | | - Work on revenue improvements and develop a continued sales action plan to increase margin and grow SOW on top accounts |

## Master the Sales Cycle

No matter what solution you sell, every sale follows roughly the same pattern. This sales cycle involves: building rapport with the customer, presenting your solution, discussing the customer's objections to your presented solution, addressing those objections, obtaining their approval, and final negotiations to obtain a commitment from the buyer. Salespeople don't often think of the stages in a sale cycle as different events. They view each step as necessary to advance the sales process. Mastering each stage is essential to sales performance success. If you're weak in one or more areas, you might still be good in the others, but you won't thrive as a salesperson. However, quite a few salespeople are challenged in one or two areas, so identifying weak points and continuing to make progress on them is vital to improving your sales results. That said, there are also situations, like Margaret's, where success factors out of the salesperson's control are missing or dysfunctional. This prolongs the sales cycle and can even lead to completely losing the deal, for no fault of the salesperson. Nonetheless, a strong understanding of the sales cycle process will help improve your management of the factors you can control and grow your win ratio.

No matter how simple or complex the deal, the entire sales cycle relies on the integration of multiple components. The salesperson needs support from other parts of the organisation to help in the presales phase and to handle fulfilment. If sales do not receive assistance from technical representatives, product managers, legal counsel, and others in the presales phase, the quality and efficiency of the sales cycle will suffer.

Depending on the sector you sell your products and services to, the sales cycle length will vary in its length, from hours to days, weeks, months, or even years. For example, the average salesperson selling a complex end-to-end IT/ICT solution in the B2B sector can close new customer acquisition deals every three to twelve months. In Margaret's case, her business development strategy enabled her to close new customer acquisition deals every four months year-on-year.

The engagement process and responsibilities for each role in the presales phase can be summed up as follows:

The Commercial Salesperson:
- Qualifies potential business opportunities and presents the value proposition, intending to close deals at an efficient rate.
- Establishes and develops a healthy sales pipeline for continued growth.
- Ensures customers are happy by resolving complaints and escalations promptly, manages the overall commercial business relationship, and retains and develops the customer's share of wallet (SOW).

The Technical Representative or Sales Engineer:
- Positions long-lasting engineering projects.
- Puts the value proposition into physical practice.
- Ensures customers are happy by providing technical insights and support around the deployment and technical implementation of the purchased solution.

## Assessing the Organisation

During twenty years of experience, I've personally encountered the complex challenges sales departments face and their possible responses to these challenges. How they handle these is important because sales is one of the most critical departments in a business. One lesson I have learned is that an assessment of their employer and its customers is a vital first step when a salesperson begins a new job. This assessment helps the salesperson understand:
- What is the overall health of the organisation, what challenges exist within it, and how does the organisation work to create the best customer experience?

- Who are the top customers? How much revenue was generated over the past three years? What products sell better than others, and which products bring in the most profit? Which regions are performing better than others, and why?
- What are the short and long-term goals of both the salesperson's organisation and the customers? Also, what action plan does each have in place to achieve these long-term goals?

Only once the salesperson has made an assessment of where they are, where they want to be, and how they will get there should they begin interacting with customers. In her case, Margaret used the ERP tool to extract customer information; she started with an assessment of where she was. Margaret would have obtained even more useful customer data and built a stronger assessment if the handover from her predecessor had taken longer than three days. It is to be hoped that your organisation offers more resources during your own handover period; if not, however, that is also something to assess. After Margaret examined the information extracted from the ERP system, she also had an overview of where she wanted to be for her next year's sales revenue target. Finally, she developed a three-year business development strategy.

## The Four Dimensions of Corporate Culture

The effectiveness of corporate culture in an organisation can be described and measured in four dimensions, which we'll call "CARD" – for Creativity, Adaptability, Responsibility, and Durability:

Creativity: One leading challenge organisations face when they want to innovate is the lack of support for new ideas. When leaders who are necessary for the implementation of an idea don't believe in it, then the innovation initiatives are destined to fail. To go from an idea to innovating the concept, you will need to include all who can be involved in the idea.

Let executives, leaders, and employees generate ideas together.

Organisations need to promote creativity in the workplace. This starts with opening our minds, looking for new possibilities, and challenging the status quo. This can include the most basic aspects of how a business is set up, even physically. For instance, an office environment's colour, lighting, sounds, and arrangement all influence how employees interact, and this is the foundation of creating thinking. Another foundation of creativity is experimenting – and we should be willing to make large changes, not to get trapped in the cycle of micro-improvements. One place our experiments can look into is disorder, because research has shown that disorder stimulates creative thinking[7]. Once new ideas are discovered and developed, creativity also helps to create buy-in. Storytelling is one way to spread ideas to touch people.

<u>Adaptability</u>: An organisation's ability to survive and make progress is determined by how effectively it adapts to change. Organisations face uncertain and chaotic environments influenced by innovation, technology, competition, regulation, and other worries that require adaptability, flexibility, and attention. This is also true on the individual scale. The demand is high for employees who need little to no supervision in carrying out their jobs and are reliable in contributing to the organisation no matter the circumstances. The most valuable employees want to be allowed to participate in problem-solving and be involved in the decision-making process on issues that concern how they can effectively do their job and achieve the organisation's goals.

An organisation must have the ability to adapt continuously and encourage employees to develop their knowledge and share it with others. This is a key way to

---

[7] https://journals.sagepub.com/doi/abs/10.1177/0956797613480186

improve performance and safeguard the survival and profit of their organisation.

<u>Responsibility</u>: While individual employees should be responsible as well as adaptable in fulfilling their duties, responsibility is even more important when it comes to leadership. The number of external and internal forces confronting organisations today have put them at a critical crossroads, which makes it necessary to re-think how they raise future leaders. Through individual experience and the media, people are becoming increasingly attuned to what constitutes a respected organisation as well as one that's a great place to work. In the most attractive companies, the leaders serve as an example. An organisation should hold leaders responsible for the corporate culture, mission statements, and intended goals, as these represent their primary tasks and express the organisation's public image. Organisation statements, however, are worthless when not lived out by the leaders who proclaim them.

<u>Durability</u>: Shared values and beliefs are durable, and they are at the heart of employees' motivation and behaviour. They are what dictate priorities and actions for change. An organisation is durable when it is also agile, able to capture lessons learned to effectively execute successive waves of change that prove scalable for the future. Periodically, opportunities for change and improvement should be considered in the following areas, the "Five Ts": (i) Teachers (leaders), (ii) Teams (people), (iii) Tools (ERP, CRM, etc.), (iv) Taste (strategy), and (iv) Tactics (processes).

## Start with the End in Mind

The biggest hidden challenge affecting corporate culture and businesses today are the disengaged employees. Research shows that seven out of every ten US workers aren't working to their full potential. This is partially because too many employees have not taken responsibility for establishing and maintaining positive attitudes and behaviours in the workplace. Therefore, the organisation's efforts to get them engaged are futile.

Products, marketing, and sales are vital to the success of every organisation, but the most valuable assets are still its people. Even with a winning product and all of the work put into developing strategies, disengaged workers cost US companies between $450 and $550 billion each year in diminished productivity.

On the other hand, employees appreciate working in an environment where they feel they are supported and can succeed. By addressing sources of disengagement, organisations protect their brand and ensure engaged employees stay engaged. According to research from Good.co, a San-Francisco-based workplace personality assessment company, organisations where a majority of employees are highly engaged experience a 19.2% improvement in operating income[8].

Creating a happy workplace is simpler said than done because happiness does not usually appear in an organisation's strategy. Unlike financial and physical assets, though, intangible assets are hard to imitate by the competition, which makes them a strong source of a competitive advantage. Therefore, measuring the value of such intangible assets is difficult, but necessary. If employees aren't happy, the organisation probably won't be successful.

In this era of globalisation and advancements in innovation, which have led to the rise of many emerging countries, it's imperative that organisations entering business with them achieve some understanding of these cultures and the businesspeople they intend to work with. They should also understand the people and cultures within their domestic regions. Employee diversity and inclusion programs are not just desirable initiatives, but have a direct impact on the organisation's bottom line. According to a

---

[8] https://www.entrepreneur.com/article/246036

McKinsey research report[9], organisations with racially and ethnically diverse workforces outperform industry norms by 35%. Another study by the Boston Consulting Group[10] revealed that companies with more diverse management teams achieve 19% higher annual earnings due to increased innovation.

No matter what your business does, creating a corporate culture that attracts and retains top employees should be a top priority.

Leaders are still challenged to find the right balance for their teams when looking for a good culture fit. Often, "fit" is what organisations say to refer to their corporate culture. The problem is, they reject hires that don't fit their corporate culture profile. For example, the hiring manager may want someone with a particular combination of skills that is hard to find, or maybe during the selection process the hiring manager thought the candidate was less approachable, or worse, there might be no true diversity programs. So, executives hire very serious people, people who have a more academic approach, but people who were more reflective and methodical are usually turned down. They miss out on the opportunity to select truly qualified candidates because of a misperception of how their own corporate culture could function with the right people in it. Another recruitment challenge is that finding the right people to scale your business is different from finding the right people to run your business.

## The Corporate Culture Strategy

Corporate culture strategies are not determined just by what some leaders say they are. Sometimes when leaders misrepresent their corporate culture, they are hiding the

---

[9]https://www.mckinsey.com/business-functions/organization/our-insights/why-diversity-matters

[10]https://www.bcg.com/en-us/publications/2018/how-diverse-leadership-teams-boost-innovation.aspx

truth; sometimes they know it but are misstating it, and sometimes they have taken a position as leaders without really knowing the reason for their organisational success. In any event, they are making a grave error by remaining narrow in their views and failing to question their assumptions or seek input from their co-workers and employees. If leaders are unwilling to listen to suggestions or consider the opinions of others, then they are not serious about establishing a happy workplace.

Productive corporate culture sources are long-lasting assets that have been constructed or discovered by an organisation over time (again, this means a competitor cannot simply duplicate these factors). Productive corporate culture has to be designed, developed, fostered, and maintained to be successful. Its design features many correlations; a productive corporate culture coordinates actions, policies, and resources to accomplish the end in mind. That said, I believe great corporate culture can only coexist in an organisation as a "decentralised construct" using holacracy and self-management.

Meanwhile, corporate culture initiatives and objectives are unsuccessful when they fail to address critical issues or when they are impracticable. Once you develop the ability to detect a toxic workplace, it will dramatically improve the effectiveness of judging, influencing, and further shaping a happy workplace (toxicity: learn to see it and stop it). A well-designed corporate culture can unlock the energy and power in every individual in an organisation. A great deal of corporate culture work is trying to figure out what is going on – not just deciding what to do, but the fundamental problem of comprehending the situation. At the same time, corporate culture is not just about what problem an organisation is trying to solve. It is about *why* and *how* they are trying to solve it. Corporate culture is primarily about deciding what is truly important and focusing resources and actions on that specific objective.

Far too many organisations, too often, do not have any corporate culture strategy. Instead, they have multiple goals and initiatives that symbolise progress but offer no way to accomplish that progress other than investing more and trying harder. An insightful reframing of a corporate culture's situation addresses new patterns of advantages or weaknesses, and a productive corporate culture strategy coordinates policy across activities, always focused on the competitive punch. It is a smart configuration of resources and actions that yield advantages in a challenging situation. Given a bundle of challenges, higher-quality resources lessen the need for a tight integration of activities. Given a set bundle of resources, there is a higher demand for smart, tight integration of those short-term resources and actions. The greater the corporate culture challenge, the higher the need for an agile, coherent corporate culture strategy. Where the corporate culture challenge is very high, it may be necessary to invest and acquire new but necessary resources for solving these challenges alongside designing a tight integration of new and existing resources and actions.

The core design of a productive corporate culture needs to be crafted as you figure out which purposes are both worth pursuing and able to be accomplished. We might look at it this way: a productive corporate culture consists of more than this core element, but if the core element is absent or distorted, then there will be a problem. Once you capture the core, it's much easier to create, describe, and evaluate a corporate culture. For instance, we can elaborate on the core element at Amazon: Zappos, which functioned as an incubator to test theories around corporate culture.

In corporate culture design, the objective is to deepen organisational skills by analysing qualitative information that focuses on key areas and provides crucial insight for the success of a culture transformation. This can be achieved through a small focus group of individuals from different parts and levels of the organisation who elaborate on how they feel about the organisation's corporate culture and their department's culture. Another approach could be one-on-one interviews with leaders and executives to gather detailed examples of the current corporate culture. Corporate culture discussion sessions, where large groups are engaged to collect feedback from more employees simultaneously, are also innovative and practical. Other approaches could be an assessment or even 180° or 360° surveys allowing employees to provide detailed feedback to executives, which is a powerful way to identify how leaders are leading the organisation. This approach measures behaviour rather than performance. Whichever tools you use, very quickly, you will come to focus on what your organisation can do more effectively than others. Looking at things from a fresh perspective will reveal many new opportunities and benefits, and identifying sources of strength and weakness will create a natural advantage. It is usually helpful to also examine the competitive environment – that is, to see what your major competitor's corporate culture may look like.

For crafting the corporate culture strategy, you need to understand and combine the following two theories on how the organisation's processes work: the leader's theory (centralised) and the employee's theory (decentralised). The employee's theory comes as a series of lessons learned and challenges amongst competing values, beliefs, and KPIs within the workplace. By contrast, the leader's theory begins with an assessment of the opportunities and threats coming from the external environment, available resources, and the amount of uncertainty and change happening. They follow a three-step process referred to as SWOT (strength, weakness, opportunities, and threats) analysis. In this process, leaders first assess their environment, their financials, their lessons learned, and other indicators that are both positive and negative. Second, they look to identify Opportunities they can work on to counteract the pain points their organisation has in its Weaknesses or Threats. For example, Margaret's challenge from day one was mainly due to the lack of a CRM tool. The Opportunity to implement CRM would have directly impacted the Threat of not having the organisation's customer data secure and safe, plus CRM tools have great value, a Strength that could lower an organisation's Weaknesses and Threats further. Third, they then select an action plan on a variety of fronts. The next step is usually to define the end in mind with the correct "fit" for your intended corporate culture image by considering the external Opportunities and internal Strengths. Concrete operational excellence objectives can be linked to the mission, vision, and overall business strategy and directly communicated to the workforce. Whichever direction your organisation ends up selecting, the SWOT analysis and following questionnaire will ensure buy-in from all parts of your organisation, with shared values and a shared view of the desired future state.

The first benefits of designing a productive corporate culture strategy come from lessons learned within the organisation. Here, get better insights by having a regional or department-based SWOT analysis conducted by a culture champion. This culture champion should be an employee who has been with the organisation for one to three years and has shown commitment to its success. Look first at the sales team, who know the ins and outs of the organisation, and ask high sales performers to complete a SWOT. My experience as a salesperson is that salespeople will usually accept an additional non-sales task if the end in mind is to create an excellent customer experience, and SWOT analyses that contribute to building a healthier corporate culture will certainly accomplish this. Once the sales department conducts their analysis, other parts of the organisation should complete theirs as well. These SWOT analyses will offer an inside-out view rather than an outside-in view of each department. After the SWOT analysis has been completed in all departments, examine the results to identify patterns that can be incorporated into the core design of your corporate culture priorities.

Another recommendation is to develop a questionnaire for executives, leaders, and employees to understand what corporate culture means to them. Find the right balance of ten to fifteen questions with multiple choice answers to identify patterns in their values, interests, and beliefs. Corporate culture represents many different things to different people in different parts of the organisation. One wants to get the feeling of its significance to each individual in an organisation. When you learn your employees' perspectives on corporate culture, only then will it be meaningful to take specific actions towards culture change and transformation in the workplace. The questionnaire will allow you to determine the norms within the organisation as a whole and in different subunits.

As you develop the employee questionnaire, use descriptions of specific actions. Focus on transparency, and be open for new ideas. Below are only four examples, taken from the internet, of what some organisations and their employees have identified as the core of a happy workplace. Try writing such a statement yourself. The goal is to identify patterns, select desired outcomes, and set these specific objectives as time-bound priorities that both leaders and employees are comfortable with and confident about achieving. Your first step is to complete the following sentence: *At the CORE of our happy workplace...*

1. _____ is a motivated and engaging workforce that thrives in the workplace and lives and breathes the organisation's ambition.
2. _____is the way that we identify and develop our leaders as a source of strength.
3. _____are outstanding processes supported by effective technology.
4. _____is good governance.

You can use some of the most common employee expectations, listed in the table on the next page, when looking for multiple-choice answers for your questionnaire. These can be categorised as objectives or outcomes.

| Allow employees to speak up; learn to listen to them | Collaborate rather than isolate |
|---|---|

| | |
|---|---|
| Show transparency in communication | Nurture a diverse workforce |
| Empower, trust, and encourage employees | Encourage team connection |
| Engage and develop employees | Establish a strong team relationship |
| Handle conflicts promptly | Ensure culture is unified throughout the organisation |
| Help leaders and employees overcome the fear of change | Integrate innovation to make job success easier |
| Offer flexibility | Outline expectations |
| Promote trust | Provide feedback regularly |
| Remove hierarchies | We reward employees for successful outcomes |

Today we see many organisations offering sales performance services to their customers. These services companies do an excellent job for an organisation's sales department performance. However, sales performance assessments or training for salespeople is not a guarantee for improving an organisation's overall performance; it is part of a series of actions. In other words, there is no doubt that it makes sense in many cases for companies to use these sales performance services, but in others, one must ask: is sales performance really an organisation's biggest challenge, or is the corporate culture challenge impacting the organisation's sales performance? Salespeople do not fail because of experience, intellect, or skills, but many fail due to the organisation's conflicting KPIs and corporate culture.

Corporate cultures are organisations' messages to the world, and we all play a part in them. Let a well-designed corporate culture strategy send a strong message of character and empathy for new hires. Are you up for it – to challenge the status quo of your corporate culture to increase your earnings by as much as 50% or more?

# Epilogue

You are at the end of the book, which means you now have a better understanding of the challenges salespeople may face in large organisations, along with the success factors needed to achieve sales revenue quotas and KPIs. You have witnessed how the engagement of each employee contributes to an organisation's business development performance and the quality of the workplace as a whole, for better or worse. Like Margaret, you are on the path to becoming a stronger salesperson with a better-established personal brand than you were yesterday. I have shared both Margaret's story and lessons learned from my own experience as a business developer and strategist.

This book describes the most extreme case of a toxic workplace that I have known to evolve in an organisation. Margaret was lucky to have never contemplated suicide, and she hopes with this book to ease the healing process for others who have experienced similar toxic workplaces. There will always be despisers of corporate culture who practice misconduct, and these can have a severe toll not just on the careers of the people who encounter them, but on the organisation's long-term survival, and in turn the job security of its employees. This book is intended to be a step in the process of identifying how corporate culture research can expand further, helping employees and organisations gain a competitive advantage as well as contributing to the overall wellbeing of our workplace society.

When sales colleagues learned that I was writing a book about corporate culture, many shared their stories of a happy workplace versus a toxic workplace. I choose to write about Margaret because she experienced the most extreme toxic workplace from my point of view, plus she quantified the value of corporate culture. However, stories from many other sales colleagues were equally important, and their understanding and motivations for establishing a happy workplace were similar to Margaret's. In any case, nobody can erase both the positive and negative workplace experiences of salespeople in their organisations, nor can anyone erase the value Margaret quantified for corporate culture: as much as 50% or more. Above all, Margaret demonstrated integrity towards her organisation's best interests over those of her manager.

Too often, employees get discharged or are set up for failure because others don't embrace their value. As a salesperson, Margaret identified four building blocks for a pledge about her character. She called it TICH – for transparency, integrity, commitment, and honesty, which you have seen in action throughout her story. In her opinion, she was discharged because the leadership didn't value her TICH pledge. In the end, though, Margaret's commitment as a salesperson still allowed her to overachieve her KPIs.

In the beginning, it was hard for Margaret to forget the unpleasant experience, but as she told her story, it helped her in the healing process. Now, she has moved on, and she doesn't know what happened to Brad, Rachael, Paul, or Elias in the meanwhile, though she likes to think that they are each living a happy life. Margaret did later learn that after she was discharged, the organisation implemented several recommendations she had proposed. Margaret has remained in sales, and while it's clear that the organisation and the group were not ready for someone like her, she is more valued in her sales role now, and she is living a much healthier life. After Margaret got discharged, she came to believe that when it happened, it was about time, because she had achieved what she came to do. She had accomplished her mission to bring stability and business development, including raising awareness of the opportunities, risks, and threats to the organisation. From there, an organisation has to keep building on lessons learned and evaluate productive corporate culture initiatives.

The moral of the story is: standing up against the abuse of power it worth the fight, even if you go in alone, and it is also worth sharing your experience later by speaking or writing about it. The point is not solely about Brad's misconduct or intentions; it is about the people whose errors or inaction also helped Brad build upon an already toxic workplace. Unfortunately, the "Bystander Effect" still happens more often than one might think. There were many moments where bystanders could have stopped the toxicity, even before Margaret worked with the organisation. Yet the bystanders decided it wasn't worth the fight for Miriam, and why would it be worth the battle for Margaret?

Another moral of Margaret's story is that we need to change the way we interpret failure. Wherever a failure exists, an equal opportunity arises. For instance, this book would not have come to life if a source like Margaret wasn't brave enough to tell her story of how she quantified corporate culture as a competitive asset.

We should intervene by speaking up and taking action when we see behaviours are inappropriate. Whichever other sources are applied to achieve a happy workplace, I believe this book provides the base upon which to build a corporate culture transformation initiative within an organisation. Also, take this manuscript as a learning experience; use it as you move forward in helping combat the workplace abuse of power, with the hope that more organisations will see it as a fight worth winning. As we have seen, in over thirty months the right workplace could deliver a 54.45% earnings increase, or the contrary, see 54.45% of their potential earnings be lost.

It is now your task to create your individual pledge as a salesperson and re-evaluate your character, values, and habits in the effort to contribute to making your workplace happier and healthier. Will you and your leadership team be up for the challenge?

# About the Author

Marcus Deiss is a business development strategist and a non-fiction author. In the past twenty-five years, he's had the opportunity to meet thousands of working professionals from different business sectors in Switzerland and across Europe, where he evaluated theories around sales performance. Simultaneously, he read books on strategic business execution and sales performance strategies. These contributed to his twenty-years track record while working in different sales roles with Fortune 500 organisations, large enterprises (LE), and small and medium-sized enterprises (SME), where he amassed a total combined sales revenue in three-digit millions of dollars.

Marcus has a real passion for business development performance. He is recognised as an expert in business development strategies, a coach, and a trainer. His award-winning experience includes building innovative service packages and strategic business development programs while working with startups and large enterprises. He is a results-driven sales professional in strategic business development and customer relationship management, primarily in the areas of information and communications technology, digital signage, and passenger information systems for mass transit. Marcus helps organisations improve sales revenue performance by applying a well-designed business development strategy with best-practice sales methods from specific industry sectors.

# Acknowledgments

Finally, a dedication: Those I love, know that I love them. I dedicate this book to humanity with sentiment, respect, and gratitude. If this book is a success, I dedicate it to my student followers and my colleagues. Further, I am grateful to and humbled by authors, journalists, and union workers, as well as all salespeople, coaches, consultants, trainers, and speakers who directly and indirectly contributed to and influenced this work, especially those who documented their findings to build the foundations of evidence upon which I could write this manuscript. I wish to thank all those who provided encouragement and were supportive along this amazing journey, including offering the opportunity to grow in the process as they challenged my thinking with critical eyes but open minds. This book is based on research conducted on the corporate culture evolution from 1997 to the present.

# Unacknowledgements

If the book is not a success, I dedicate it to despisers of corporate culture who practice misconduct in their workplaces, along with all those bystanders who enable toxic workplaces to prosper.